Pearls for Girls
Dating, Waiting & Sex

Pearls for Girls
Dating, Waiting and Sex

In Seeking Cupid,
Don't be Stupid!

by

RICHARD ALAN NAGGAR

Edited and Published

by

KATHLEEN MARIE BROWN

First Edition

2011

Inside Cover Illustration:
Canadian Geese
by Thea Brown

This edition published in 2011 by
Brown Publishers

Printed in the United States of America

ISBN 978-0-615-44234-1

Regarding the subject of dating, waiting and sex...

*   ...to those of you who have tried (and are tired) of all the world's systems, who have followed the advice of well-meaning family and friends, who have been duped and tricked by unseen forces, or have been plain foolish and ignorant because you have never traveled this way before,*

*   I dedicate this book.*

-    *Richard Alan Naggar*

TABLE OF CONTENTS

III. IDENTITY

IV. DATING

V. COURTING, LOVE, MARRIAGE, DIVORCE

Preamble

Hello there and welcome to your beautiful life....I will be your host throughout this book. This book is about you, your wants, desires, and your pursuit of happiness in the seeking of a companion. I want you to have the optimum experience. I hope to offer clarity, meaning, and purpose on the subject of dating, courting, sex, and marriage, as it pertains to women of all ages. The book is one giant submittal for the reader's approval and use...yet the reader does not remain the same upon laying it down afterwards. My purpose is to gently remind you that your heart's desires are not a myth or an unattainable dream in a faraway place. No. What we are searching for is right here, accessible to us, with little or no effort, and is free to those who want it. The result is nothing less than a premium life experience which far exceeds anything money, power, or fame can provide. In fact, those that have everything would do well to read this book. They may be surprised to find out that the essence of true love is made up of ingredients from those that participate fully in it. Let all the butterflies that are found fluttering around in your stomach be put on notice...we now have a worthy mission on our hands and worlds to conquer. Where I mention the word *girls*, I'm also referring to young ladies and women. Age references go from 13 to 60, and I have scattered data for all ages throughout, for your consideration. The mention of a mate, pal, companion, friend and partner, also stand in for each other. Where God is mentioned, it includes the powers that be, Creator, life-giver and the origin of all things.

This is the book the men in your life who love you, like your good dad, brother, uncle or cousin, would want you to read, while the other male types out there, those who want to use you, would hope you'll never see. This is not a religious book, but a spiritual one, with a specific theme: God and *YOU*...the woman he created. This book serves up generous helpings of truths, insights, and uplifting statements, coupled

1

with my sincere desire that the still voice within you will be stirred up. My deepest wish is that you learn how to fish…to cast out your net, haul it in, keep the best fish and throw the rest back, and eventually become the fisher of one man.

I use spiritual principles to make some of my points. I strongly recommend that you allow God to guide your heart on these subjects and your true life will follow. What you will find here, honors all people who seek truth, meaning, inner growth, and closure. Love is included. Let us begin, my dear Reader.

I will see you amongst the stars and beyond, and will know you by the sparkle in your eye.

- *Richard Alan Naggar*

Girl Pearl: *Men who love truth, righteousness and fair play, usually love women with all their hearts. Women, in return, cannot help but love the one who sent him…to her.*

2

Preface

Dear girls and lovely ladies of all ages: If the subject of love either attracts or repels you, *Pearls for Girls* is the book for you. This book's inner-parts will stir *your* inner-parts, and teach you things you've never heard. I'm speaking to the pure-hearted, the broken-hearted and the hard-hearted. How often does a book come along that captures and supports the feminine perspective, and offers the insights of a man who has your best interest at heart no matter what life has dealt you prior to this moment? What price can one place on that? *Richard Alan Naggar* is that man, and *Pearls for Girls* is that book. It speaks without compromise, reservation, or sappiness, yet is gentle and mild in the doing of it. It gives valuable insights into the world of men, and causes women to take stock of their feminine natures at the same time. As you venture *inward* toward self-examination during the dating process, you'll be looking *outward*, making silent *notes to self*, becoming aware, and never doubting what you see and hear. How often we can say in hindsight that we were given warning signs early in our relationships, yet overrode them and chose our own way instead. Once you key-in to the insights and observations this book offers, you cannot *help* but practice them wherever you go, reaching even beyond the dating world and into the fascinating and endless world of people.

The beautiful pearls you are bound to discover will present you with matters for the heart to weigh and consider. Identity, virtue and choosing rightly, all lead to those crossroads in life that will play out their corresponding rewards or consequences, and one day show us who we are. Throughout the book is a gentle voice that will summon you forward toward truth, while it calls you back from danger. *Pearls for Girls* is a door standing open before you with a gracious invitation to come inside for a journey of self-revealing intimacy that enlightens, compels, then prepares any willing woman for her original occupation, that is, *company to man....*the right man, that is! If you're looking for love, dear woman, turn the page...

- Kathleen Marie Brown

3

I. GENERAL DISCUSSION

The Author

Imagine what your life would be like if someone was watching out for your best interest and making you his concern, full-time and nonstop. Regardless of how you grew up and what happened along the way, you got here, and you are here now. Starting in this moment, we will take on the pleasant task of seeing that things go right, well and good, using what God has set up so brilliantly within us. If you allow me, I will be your good dad, granddad, uncle, brother, protector, neighbor, friend, guide and counselor on the subjects of dating, waiting and sex. Perhaps I will just be the one you want to listen to. At the very least, my feedback and input will compliment your beliefs and your current walk in life. Get excited, because we're about to do great things!

Girl Pearl:
*What a strange thing is man! And what a stranger
is woman! What a whirlwind is her head, and what a
whirlpool full of depth and danger is all the rest about her.*
- Byron

Questions

For some of you, this may become the best part of the book. You see, in one book I cannot cover all the dynamics of your personal issues on various subject matters. Considering that no two people are alike, feedback and input, specialized to the individual, is not only necessary, but preferred. For that reason, an email address is included with this book. Because we do not know each other, and will probably never meet, we may find ourselves freer to explore some pretty sensitive subjects, some of which I've covered. I am extending an invitation to you

4

to share your questions or problems, with the understanding I will give input and feedback, but you will make your own decisions on what you do. Your common sense must be awakened first, then listened to, and finally acted on by you. However, I do promise to stir your inner parts. From there, you must journey.

No subject is too hot to handle. I suggest getting right to the point and being as clear as you can. You may also choose to remain anonymous. I do not collect or distribute personal data and have no desire to do so. What is important is that you get an answer and then do as you will. To discover something by it being self-evident is the highest learning form on this planet. The answer is within you. Let's flush it out.

Girl Pearl: In the passing of time, I knew not the true value of love until my love was taken for granted.

Taking God Out

You can remove God from this subject and the suggested methods will still work, but I highly recommend you do not do so. The Creator of all things, the one who commands the molecules and beyond, is someone you want on your side in everything you do. The Old Testament proves the point very well. When God is with you, you prevail; if he's not, the story has a different ending. False lives, thwarted destinies and wrong paths abound. Ladies, we need his help and guidance. Please, not only ask and seek for it, but follow the gentle inner instructions as they unfold in and through you. Develop a prayer life. This starts by faith, believing you are known, your needs are known, and that you were deliberately invited to be here. Share with your heavenly Father and he will lend you his ear and counsel every time!

By allowing God to join you, very interesting things happen. Many situations will tend to flow in your favor. Quite a few will protect you and direct your path to safety. I have often shared the difference between God being in one's life or not, in this humorous way: those who have some belief in God tend to get flat tires in their driveways, or around the corner from work or home. Those who don't, have another destiny. There will always be the risk of getting a flat, but be clear that every occurring incident is growth being submitted to you. The point is, *how* we learn our lessons is as important as the lessons themselves.

Instructions, lessons, and answers may not come as you expect them to, so be an open receiver to whatever comes your way. To illustrate the point, "We pray for courage, then danger comes so that courage might be. We ask for wisdom, but receive trouble, so that wisdom might come. We pray for love, but receive torment, so that love will reply. Why is it we complain then, that our prayers are not being heard and answered?" You get the picture? God's thoughts and our thoughts are not the same, and your answers will come in ways you know not. Therefore, be aware and ready for whatever comes, don't miss anything, and rejoice in what comes. When God joins us, the impossible is no longer with us, lies and deception cannot have their way, and the desires of the heart begin to materialize.

Girl Pearl: Don't seek the relief that permits you to forget your suffering, and, at the same time, allows you to forget God. Go toward the suffering that cleanses your soul.

The Theme of This Book

This book takes the way of the narrow road, the road less traveled. It promotes customs and traditions based on man/woman relationships intended to endure, prosper and find favor with God and man. It encourages the short-term pain that comes about from seeking answers to relevant questions, until one discovers the long-term pleasure of the favored answers. I am in favor of marriage, abstention from sex during dating and courting (read the whole book), and finishing what you start. (Again, read the whole book.)

"Pick one and settle down" is my mantra. This is what I'd hope to see happen for you. The moral climate in today's world on this subject is broken and corrupt, and its practice not only prolongs its dysfunction, but keeps its followers in a place of compromise, ambiguity and weakness. Until we discover what to do, as well as how to do it, using faith as we journey is a wise thing to do. In addition, practice not being willful with the subjects of dating and marriage. Willfulness produces frustration, which leads to anger, resentment, and depression. Skip all that and keep it light and fun. You want to be interested in this subject, but not desperate for an outcome. Faith defined: *believing without seeing*. Faith, when properly applied, can do just about anything.

May I suggest that you do not memorize, as much as familiarize yourself with this book. You see, I want to awaken the powers, skills, and talents already inside you, waiting to serve you. I'm hoping this book stirs you, causes you to ask questions, and contemplate just what you're doing and why…that is the power of the book. It joins and compliments your common sense, and from there you will know what to do to seek and discover your personal optimum. My hope is that you learn and apply important issues of life without experiencing them the hard way, sampling them frivolously, or allowing them to have their way with you. My other hope is to preserve your inner child and your innocence during the dating process.

If, like everyone, you've made some poor decisions, I will address how to clean all that up and start anew. One last thing: I submit all this for consideration and contemplation. I am not forcing any particular way on you. The optimum experience is submitted for you to take in, reject, or select. Take what I have said, and add it to your own inner treasures. Find your comfortable place in the whole scheme of things. Now, I will let the younger girls and women in on a little secret that the more mature women already know and would agree with. Life is brief. For some mysterious reason, it drags in the beginning, and you find yourself wanting to speed it up. Then, just as you begin to figure things out, life accelerates and you find yourself wishing it would slow down. This phenomenon is at work on everyone. There are many roads to travel here on this earth and no two of them are alike. Apply yourself, seek your true destiny, and do not settle for less. Time will take on a different meaning when you are in pursuit of quality instead of quantity. Perhaps you will suffer in this process, but it will be for the right reasons, and taking the time to find the right way for you is well worth it. Your portion has been set aside by the Creator and is set up so that only you can claim it. Please do, my dear ladies.....please do.

Girl Pearl: *She is pretty to walk with, and witty to talk with,*
And pleasant too, to think on.
- Sir John Suckling

Girl Pearl: *Woman, I tell you, is a microcosm; and rightly to*
rule her, requires as great talents as to govern a state.
- Samuel Foote

Girl Pearl: *There is a woman at the beginning of all great things.*
- Lamartine

II. ALL ABOUT YOU

The First Recorded Non-Date

Adam and Eve did not date, nor did they wait to get married. Sex came naturally, and their Cupid was not stupid. But then, look who was in charge. No less than the Creator of all things, and the Author of love itself. Since then, everything has gone in other directions for the human race. The intimate coming together of two people has become more complex and liberal, is marketed for profit, fun and function, and then left to happenstance. This subject cannot be left to chance or good intentions, and then be expected to turn out successfully. It requires responsible and accountable handling. In today's society, girls and women of all ages can be at a disadvantage when it comes to finding a husband. I sense that the needs of the female population are not being met in a fulfilling and satisfying way. The American capitalistic society of life, (no criticism intended) has all but removed the courting ritual and replaced it with instant actions and shallow answers to a most serious subject. Depth, meaning and purpose have all but been eliminated or, at the very least, compromised. Instead of love being a matter of the heart as it should be, it has become a matter of the intellect, emotions and five senses. No wonder, as a society, we are having so much trouble with this. The true spirit of love has been given a back seat when it should be driving the vehicle. It's the application of the microwave mentality of wanting a five-star meal without having to wait for it. In love and life, this will never do.

The divorce rate in this country is currently between fifty and sixty percent, well over half of all marriages. The marriage institution has become so impoverished that many choose not to marry because they don't believe it will work. That's one way to reduce the divorce rate...the wrong way, I might add. Look what we've done, and continue to do: we've hurried the process, removed key elements of courtship, and then expected superior results. We commercialized and desensitized the intimate coming together of two people, and are now witnessing less than satisfying results. But results don't lie. In fact, these divorce rate results are proving to be very disruptive. That math will never make sense, yet we continue repeating the patterns that bring it about. Repeating something over and over, each time expecting a different result, is the definition of insanity. By admitting we may be out of our minds on this subject, we can now begin to search for, and apply, what *does* work, since we already know what doesn't. Given that we are not operating at optimum, the future remains highly questionable. Perhaps revisiting and re-examining the dating stage, then waiting (courtship) while we navigate through it, will help restore true meaning to love and marriage, or at the very least, offset this negative dynamic.

Education, or knowledge of the subject matter, plays an important role in just what statistic you turn into. People who do not finish high school, or just barely get through, are more likely to become single parents, experience less happiness, and endure a higher divorce rate than a college educated person. Becoming well-informed on the subject of marriage before making decisions, greatly improves your outcome. This dynamic plays out in just about anything you do. When buying a car for instance, research will help you enter into the subject with more data, allowing you to choose more wisely on the purchase. We have learned much about why things fail. Perhaps some dialogue on how to succeed is timely and in order. You see, marriage supports commitment and commitment supports responsibility. This is similar to the pressure that a piece of coal, or a caterpillar will endure if they are to flourish and enter into another phase of their existence, namely a diamond or a butterfly. Pressure, applied correctly and for the right reasons, will produce noble results. We are made in the image of God. If an animal was able to upgrade itself to the status of man, surely it would do so. Evolving is decidedly preferred to devolving. How then, does mankind justify choosing to devolve and become less noble? Yet this is the result when the marriage dynamic is mocked. It is a slow, downhill spiraling descent into hell. Look around you, and wherever you see the lack of commitment to other human beings, the quality of life is missing and the optimum joy, peace, and harmony are gone.

10

This generation and the generations to come, stand to be tainted to the point of toxicity unless nobility and uprightness accompany us while we travel. A solid marriage provides an environment for these virtues to grow. Practicing responsible dating and pre-dating techniques, and eliminating sex from the courting ritual, would vastly improve our marriage conditions. The systems need to be purified, flushed out, and begun again from a fresh foundation. When it comes to the subjects of marriage and meeting the needs of today's woman, nothing can be spared, trimmed, or left out. When a woman activates the songs that are in her heart, the whole world sings with her. I want to hear lots of singing.

Girl Pearl:
Then, my good girls, be more than women, wise:
at least be more than I was; and be sure
you credit anything the light gives life to
before a man. - Beaumont and Fletcher

The Difference is Women

You, the feminine mystique, are the subject of this book, and what a glorious subject you are! Time has cheapened, diluted, and distorted the origin and wonderful contributions of the true woman. A world without women doesn't make sense; a world with women whose needs go unmet doesn't make sense either. Until men address this problem by becoming more responsible stewards of the planet and all that is upon it, women may have to step up and lend a hand.

The current state of the world in regard to social growth and well-being requires a fix. Starting now, men and women who come together must learn to create a better foundation...for themselves first, then for their children, and finally for the next generation to build on. Women can begin by concentrating on their belief systems and behaviors, which must be modified, corrected, and then redirected. Ladies, take stock of yourselves. You have everything necessary to fulfill the desires of your hearts and to journey well and deep. Some of you are just starting out in the dating world, others have launched and haven't done too well, while still others are thrust back into the mix and don't know what to expect. Well, the beginning of every journey starts with a simple step...then another and another, until before long, what you are looking for comes into view. You bought the book which is a good first step. Now let's pick up the pace.

This book is catered to the female and her cause, and is biased in her favor. The author wants all women everywhere to ride into the sunset with their intendeds, and live happily ever after until death does them part. I don't want you to be hurt, taken advantage of, or taken prisoner on the way there. Until the guy in your life gets it, you are responsible for teaching and training him to recognize, then respond correctly, to your needs. So be prepared to take the lead when the opportunity is presented and called for. This book will prepare you for that.

It is not uncommon to experience a degree of resistance when reading certain parts of this book. Keep in mind that on the other side of resistance is growth. Therefore, learn to go *toward* any type of resistance and expect to claim your growth when doing so.

Girl Pearl: *A man should be as a compliment to a woman, so when they are joined, their combined value instantly doubles. Whether or not they venture higher, is up to them.*

Achieving Life Optimum

Throughout the book, the word 'optimum' will come up often. Optimum is defined as: *the most favorable conditions or greatest degree of operating under any given circumstances one can achieve or experience.* Think about this. We not only want to achieve optimum, but how about *giving* optimum too. Nothing less can be invested if you want to soar like an eagle. There is no greater existence than optimum. Taking all you possess (whatever that is) and bringing it to bear in the moment is to strive, or reach for, this experience in its fullest. Being real, genuine, honest, and forthright helps point the way. Dressing correctly and smartly, applying makeup (if any) responsibly, allowing your feminine side to rule, and activating your elegance and etiquettes, when running at optimum, will stop a room full of people, open closed doors, and clear your path of unwanted obstacles. You are that woman. When I see a woman in all her potential, running at optimum, I first give thanks to God and then to her, for she is a most pleasurable sight to behold and experience. When I see less than that, I become concerned. I want you running at optimum. The world, dark forces, and even some dysfunctional personal beliefs must be restrained, detained, retrained, and then used for your personal gain. Optimum awaits you, and you must learn to activate and use it to suck the marrow out of life, circumstances, and even the very moment you are in. Remember, we will not travel this way again. Nothing less than optimum for you, starting right now. Optimum, here I come!

Girl Pearl: Imagine you woke up one morning and you were the only one of your kind in existence. Imagine that.
Well, it is happening to you right now.

No Formula for Living

We are all born with talents and skills unique unto ourselves in different combinations. Whatever your skills bank and makeup are, you are commanded to use them, and to use them wisely. Finding an environment that reveals them and allows you to practice them, requires starting a personal journey at least, and staying vigilant at best. There are many paths in life, so *how* we learn our lessons, and *how* we live to the fullest, are not at issue. Beginning a path, then continuing on it, is.

Remember, human beings have been created to function as highly intelligent motion machines, far in advance of any other life form on this planet. Each of us is a self-contained unit that is mobile, can think on its feet and perform spectacular feats wherever it goes. At the very least, life is to be deeply lived and vastly experienced. Because we have a degree of consciousness beyond that of insects, plants and animals, allowing us to boast we are made in God's image, we are commanded, instructed and expected to carry out greater actions with what has been given to us. Let us remind ourselves that mankind was created for, and charged with, stewarding nothing less than an entire planet. A woman plays a huge role in this endeavor. Before discovering and experiencing this extraordinary life, you may find yourself dreaming about it. Good! Because we are now going to put some legs on those dreams.

As you begin to mature, you will notice choices presenting themselves to you which you've never had to entertain. In considering what to do, it is wise to learn as much as you possibly can from those who have gone before you. Why suffer unnecessarily? By learning from the mistakes of others, you will wisely enhance your own journey. It is the same with any subject. Research it, investigate it, and then apply it to your life to suit your needs and wants. Results don't lie, and lack of results don't lie either. Therefore, constant seeking and tweaking is necessary until we find what we're looking for. Beware of the road that is wide and well-traveled. It is everywhere you go. Dating is one of those roads. It is where the cattle all come together and you can't tell them apart. Although all must start out on this wide road, let it be with the understanding that you are looking for your own personal and narrow path, the one that was prepared for you from the beginning of time, before you arrived here. The carving out of this path is very intimate, and is unique only to you.

All journeys, and love is no different, come with a degree of risk....and why shouldn't they? How can there be gain without risk? We are required to play a part and God has promised to play a part too. Somehow, we continue to be reluctant, ignorant, hesitant or unavailable, not doing our parts completely, and we end up interfering with the natural process of the two coming together. Truly, we know not what we do. We need help and guidance, and we need them in abundance. What makes our journeys even more intriguing is that we are under the sentence of time, which contributes an interesting dynamic to the whole picture. Think of a game show, where you have only a matter of seconds to reach for, and secure the grand prize. When time is up, either you won it or you didn't. Second prize and booby prizes are available, but why settle for them when you can have what is truly yours? Ladies, use your time wisely to get it. *My* goal is to prepare you for *your* goal, that is, the grand prize.

Girl Pearl: Save the love we pay to heaven, there is none purer, holier, than that a virtuous woman feels for him she would cleave through life to. Sisters part from sisters, brothers from brothers, children from their parents, but such a woman from the husband of her choice, never! - Knowles

Adam was Speechless

What do you give someone who has everything? This question has plagued millions of people throughout the centuries. The little drummer boy (Pahrump pum pum pum) gave something to the king that brought him great joy because it was something the king did not have, nor could he buy. He gave *himself,* and gave all that he had in doing so. What he gave from the heart was received by the heart. The purest of all gifts originate there...in the heart. Listen to the lyrics of the Little Drummer Boy song, because they explain the gift and its effect on all who heard it. It was more than sufficient...so much so,

15

that even the animals liked it, the people's hearts melted, and it eventually helped the king find the humility required to become a better king. In another story, the poor widow in the Bible, who gave two shekels, was credited as giving the most prized gift in the room. She, too, gave all she had. Those who give all they have, give gifts of extreme value. They, themselves, are the true gifts, for they are sharing themselves.

As for Adam, once the God of all things and Creator of all universes, had given Adam an entire planet and all that was upon it, what did he add to this already magnificent experience? *A woman.* The crowning glory, the parting thought and the finishing touch of one of the most riveting times in creation. Let this sink in.

Adam didn't even know what he wanted or what to ask for, but he sure recognized it when he saw Eve.

You see, God knows how to give good gifts before you ask, even before you *know* what you want! Woman, you are that good gift. In being introduced to creation, Adam had been non-stop observing and receiving experiences he could never have conceived or imagined. The greatest surprise, however, was saved for last. Eve: his compliment, companion, helpmate, intimate and like-kind, bone of his bone and flesh of his flesh, perfectly designed for, and fit for him. I can easily hear Adam's heart say: *Oh, thank you, Lord,* and I also have to believe that when he said it, it really meant something. I want those words to mean something in your life today, as well.

Girl Pearl: When woman was created, the desire of Adam's heart was fulfilled.

Less is More

Girls, what you will discover as you read throughout this book, is that when you do the work suggested, your own personal stock as a human being will go up. When it does, it will come about in a subtle way, almost undetectable as it unfolds. Other people may even see the results before you do. This means that over time you will become more valuable as a human being, both to yourself and to the world around you. You may notice little changes such as partying less, and devoting time to more serious and worthy ventures. You will notice that less effort by you will produce more results in just about anything you do, hence the paradox. In time, you will learn that wherever you go, there you are, and you are either complete and content, or incomplete and disconnected. Negative and destructive behaviors, those that are not benefiting your life, must be unlearned and cast off before you can begin learning a higher way to proceed. You will stand out from the crowds. You will not belong to the cattle drives or herds of people falling over each other for false love and approval in all the wrong ways. No, not you. You will become like gold. The value of gold is assigned to it for what it takes to acquire it. Manpower, time, energy, and money all go into mining gold in large quantities. Even when only a little is produced, its value is high because of the effort involved. You are that valuable nugget when you go out there and apply yourself correctly. The mother lode remains in you to be mined over time, as you journey. In this new world of womanhood you'll be creating for yourself, you'll begin to attract something in the world that, like gold, is very worthwhile, hard to find, but still available: a true man. This true man is looking for an extraordinary catch: a true woman. Like attracts like. This woman will be pursued, wanted, cherished, loved and sought after. In doing your part correctly, it is not uncommon to have several men inquiring after you, all vying for your affections. Your most difficult task will be having to eventually choose one and settle down. This, however, will not be until you are sure, ready, and have tested your feelings and his, and the timing is right. It will present itself in due course, as you continue to progress. You will not be attracted to ani-males any longer, as you have done your homework. You'll no longer be merely a female (least highest form), but on your way to becoming a true woman. This will cause you to have more free time on your hands, because you will have learned to be discriminatory with your time and efforts. You will get more in return for less effort. Why? Because being yourself requires little or no effort at all. Being other than yourself requires maintenance...that is, energy spent where it could have been stored or used elsewhere. To be or not to be has always been the question. Now you have the answer. Ladies, make no mistake about it. Turn on the inner lights and functions, and the outer can't help but shine bright and far. That is what we are going to do here. Be anxious for nothing, and expect everything.

Girl Pearl: *It's not the beauty you show, but the beauty showing you that matters.*

Losing Your Innocence

Have you noticed how everyone lights up when babies are mentioned or introduced? Sure you have. Even a pregnant women exudes a joy, a radiance that, while you can't actually *see* the innocence, it's wrapped all around her like a garment.

18

The happy moment arrives and out pops another newborn. Pure, unblemished innocence, delivered into your hands for ultimate care. So, how is it that we come into the world so sweet, then somehow, somewhere along the way, get tainted? What happens to that child from the time it is born, up to the point it matures? Some*thing* is trying to steal its innocence, and it never stops trying.

We don't lose innocence all at once, or even in a single act, which is a common misconception. No, it empties out over time, and becomes something of a leakage that creates a vacuum (or void) where other things, not so innocent, can enter. When the leakage is stopped, we can begin the process of recapturing what was lost. This is universal, and applies to every human being ever born, and is why we need a savior who can help us return from our fall and get back to our purpose and most favored condition: innocence. Take heart, because what was lost can be found, what was stolen can be regained, what was not known will be revealed, and there is a way to go about triggering it all. (Please consult the Repentance chapter.)

As we come into this world pure and innocent children, we would do well to exit the same way. There are forces in this world that prefer you don't succeed, but they do not have the final say. *You* do, thanks be to God. Those forces will work against you and your entire family. Some can be seen coming and others are invisible, but they exist and have an agenda. Well, so do we, and ours is powered by heaven. A good start is to renounce resentment and judgment; to do nothing counter to life, liberty, and the well-being of others; to display charity when offered the opportunity; to be mindful of, and grateful for, what you have and how you came to have it; to finish the task assigned to you, whether it be in marriage, with children, or a commitment; to seek the right, the pure and the just way in any given moment...this is your best at work, and it is good to be found working.

Life can be like driving a car and coming to a turn. Make the turn, then straighten out the wheels. Be aware that mistakes will visit you to teach you lessons. Life's school of discipline will continue until your last day, and then school is out, and what you did will be your testimony. Learn your lessons with a heart of gratitude and not sourness. You may be knocked down or forced to abruptly turn left or right, but get back up, pick up the pieces, and come back to your center at the end of each episode. Expect no guarantees, but have hope and look for good fortune and opportunity, not for yourself only, but for others as well. Remember that the other person has not been here before either, and is fighting daily battles just like you. Lend a hand if you can, and if you can't, try not to hinder anyone along the way. Leave the same way you came in, which is with all your innocence intact. Let the child in you chart the course with your adult supervising. Travel well and deep.

Girl Pearl: Don't be in a hurry for anything...instead, make the wait worthwhile.

20

Growing Up Too Quickly...Don't

...And if you did, let's work on either stopping or reversing the process. This can apply to anyone between the ages of thirteen to sixty. We want to become more like little children, receivers and observers of life, cast out worry, fear, confusion, and doubt, and take rest and gratitude in the moment, for all we've been given. Society prompts us to move better, faster and cheaper, and it takes its toll on us. Nothing less than our highly prized innocence is at stake. If you have ever seen someone who has lost their innocence, then you understand what I'm referring to. The loss of it doesn't look good on any soul, at any age.

Everything has its timing, and there is a natural flow to life if we sail with its current. Human beings are designed to process what comes naturally in its own time, and not before. Being forced to do anything is not the way to bring out your true self. Girls, activating some of the psychological, emotional, or mental aspects of your psyche before their appointed times can be stressful and counterproductive. Oh, it can be done, but it is not necessarily in the flow of life. Go with the natural pace of things. Don't hurry or be anxious for anything. Everyone gets to experience the desires of their hearts, but learning to enjoy them is another story. Pre-dating is a valuable option to consider in finding your way slowly and thoughtfully into the world of dating. Be aware, take your time, and let's see what develops for you.

Girl Pearl: Visualize the man you want to be with, the people you want to meet, the places you want to go, and the job you want to have. Then, don't dwell on it. While the requests are being worked on, work on yourself to receive them.

Virgins: Gather Ye Rosebuds While Ye May

The interpretation of this poem inspires to this very day, and yes, this was a poem addressed to *virgins* as an exhortation to make the most of time....their time and their youth. Of course in today's world and interpretations, it applies to non-virgins as well. The inference to the reader from the author, Robert Herrick, included our potential to be here today, but possibly not tomorrow. The point is made to not waste the time allotted to you, however much that is. It inspires *carpe diem,* or *seize the day.*

> Gather ye rosebuds while ye may,
> Old time is still a-flying:
> And this same flower that smiles today
> tomorrow will be dying.
>
> Then be not coy, but use your time,
> And while ye may, go marry:
> For having lost but once your prime,
> You may forever tarry.

What it means is to marry while the beauty of youth remains, making the most of your time. By not gathering your rosebuds (opportunities), you miss them, and herein lies the point: time and mystery wait for no one, so make the most of each moment. We are motivated to leap into life while we can, remembering that people validate people, making the world go round, and giving meaning to life. Whether in groups, families or as individuals, human souls remain the most valuable asset on the planet. With them comes enormous responsibility as well. Start with yourself, then begin to help others.

Girl Pearl: *When we were born, school of life started; when we die, school is out.*

People Transmitting and Receiving

Seeing that human souls are the most valuable asset on the planet, it follows that profitable dialogue is the most wholesome and nourishing *food* for the human soul. It not only invites profound meaning into life, it has the unexpected benefit of weeding out the insincere or false elements in human beings, to keep us from being attracted to the wrong types of people. Try it. Bring up meaningful dialogue and watch what happens to people around you. Some will respond by making a joke, others will quickly change the subject, and still others will not respond at all, or make a quick exit. As you become an observer, the experiences you see become your teachers. Start making sense, and people with no sense move on. Good!

Clear communication is the responsibility of the communicator. In any relationship, we must aim to connect, dialogue, and have no secret thoughts from each other. Deliberate efforts must be made. The question to ask ourselves is: *are we talking "with" or "at" each other?* Honest, clear discourse will not fail you when employed. This may be difficult if you were raised in a home where dialogue and communication were avoided or discouraged. So, when learning to speak up rather than hold things in, it may be awkward at first, and the right words may not flow too well. Your heart may be engaged, but the brain and mouth do not cooperate. Realize this is normal, and that your communication skills will improve with usage. During this learning process, it is not uncommon for some to stutter, go blank or get flustered. Resist the temptation (the easy way out) to hold things in and glide out of the moment without expressing yourself and getting your needs met. Risk saying and doing what is in your heart, and this path will lead you to discover and strengthen your identity, as well as bolster your self-esteem. It may be awkward, embarrassing or cause discomfort, but this is the ante in the world of personal growth. When it happens, simply realize the pain of the moment and move on. Your lesson will be learned and preserved, and you'll advance to the next moment's lesson. One effective and sure-fired way to get some practice communicating is to become a good listener. People like to talk. This is your opportunity to

23

listen and learn. Not only will you learn about yourself, but simultaneously you'll be learning about the other person. Encourage the speaker with your attentiveness until you are ready to jump in and share yourself. Life awaits you, and being a good listener is not hard to do.

A good way to test your communication skills is to describe a peanut butter sandwich. Do you begin with the wheat that grows in the fields, is ground into dough, then baked into bread? Do you start with going to the market to buy a loaf? Is the peanut butter chunky or is it plain? You get the picture? Explain what you want the other person to experience. Leave something out and you leave it to chance. On the other hand, in contributing too much detail, you risk losing your audience. Being observant of others' facial expressions and responses to your description, will give you a good indication of whether you're holding their attention or have lost them in detail. As to reading a particular situation, body language is very revealing, and can be useful, keeping in mind it is not an exact science. There are males with hidden agendas whom, when you look them in the eye, waiver, drift, look away, falter or stutter. Good. We need to find out what is going on inside a person. Take note of this when it happens. Your confidence level will bring this out. People who are open and honest, use open body and eye contact. Those who are closed, cross their arms and legs. People who are confused or considering what you're saying, cover their mouths. People who are listening are still and focused, and not fiddling around. Study up on body language to have a better awareness. It is a fascinating subject and you will even glimpse yourself in the process!

Your goal is to learn to clearly state what you mean. Speaking with conviction (without doubt) is equally important to clear communication. Your *no* must mean *no,* and your *yes* must mean *yes.* Practice being clear, courteous, and precise, without doubt, confusion or ambiguity in your delivery. If you are not clear, your listener certainly won't be either. Send your message, then check to see if it was received. When it has been received, it is your turn to listen. Let your ear grow twice the size, look the person in the eye, don't fiddle with your fingers, and listen attentively. There is power in that process for both the giver and the receiver.

Girl Pearl: You cannot outsource the work required to become a better person. That work defines your character, and that is what makes you...you!

My Way or the Highway

Married or dating couples spend more time arguing redundantly and never resolving issues, because neither one knows or takes time to identify what the issues really are. I am not talking about the little things that come up and can be laughed at or shrugged off. I am talking about the issues that need to be discussed. Failure to communicate produces an elephant in the room, that people pretend is not there. Heck, rather than deal with them, some people give them pet names. I have actually walked into homes where there were so many elephants roaming around I thought I was in India or Africa. In other words, problems abounded and people got used to that being their normal condition. This is living at minimum rather than optimum, and is borderline dysfunction. In approaching any disagreement, never blame or believe it is the other person who is the entire problem. Start with yourself. Also, as you begin to speak, keep to only one issue. Multiple issues cannot be resolved all at once, and become overwhelming to both parties. To make sure you are being heard and understood, the following tools are recommended:

Once you have stated your issue, request that the other person repeat back what you said. Then, listen carefully to the answer. This is called feedback, and it's good stuff. The person will *feed back* to you, your own words as they understood them. Don't be shocked when you hear you didn't hit your mark. Be relieved you got clarity and that the misconception was outed,

25

then just have another go at it. In this process, ninety percent of the problem will be corrected and resolved. Resist the temptation to argue or repeat what did not work, but instead leap on the second opportunity to go again, clean it all up, and be heard. Remember, we are seeking connection first, and then resolution. Next, make your statements brief and to the point, pausing to make inquiries such as: *Does that make sense? Are you tracking with me? Would you like further clarity? May I proceed?* Avoid the ranting and soap opera dramas during this process.

When the other person's turn comes to respond, your opportunity has arrived to practice silence, patience, empathy and genuine interest in the speaker. You may not agree with what is being said, but listening and being courteous while doing so, encourages open, honest dialogue, and produces an environment conducive to trust and openness. Nodding your head indicates your attentiveness, and eye contact cements the moment. Consider that being listened to and understood is a very gratifying experience. As simple as it seems to accomplish, many do not know how to initiate or sustain this process. Not everyone with a mouth and ears knows how to use them. Once a person feels they've been truly understood and paid attention to, they begin to recognize the value of the process, and often feel compelled to eagerly return the gesture. In this way, the issue is identified, sent, acknowledged, and returned, and the two have truly practiced communicating and understanding each other. Repeat the process with every issue until all elephants have been removed from the room. Now we are going places and sucking the marrow out of life, living the dream instead of living *in* a dream. Remember, practice makes perfect, and everything takes time. Enjoy the learning curve and expect great results.

Girl Pearl: Remember, Prince Charming has to be trained to be the man you want him to be...which is the work of a Princess!

Habits: Good, Bad & Dysfunctional

As habits root themselves in the subconscious mind and become automatic responses, we begin to practice them via our second nature (without thinking). It is a form of programming and can be detrimental when it comes to staying in the moment and creating the growth necessary to find and become our true selves. Mental, emotional, spiritual, physical, and psychological realms all want to eat and be fed. These categories are what make up your life and define you as a person. Habits we form in each of these groups, can benefit us or slowly destroy us, depending upon how stringently we adhere to them. We must be on guard against becoming so strong in our ways that we remain unreachable and stay that way. That's why when disagreeing with someone, be open to the possibility of modifying your position, should it be warranted. Remember, whatever it is you argue adamantly for, without giving in, you will be allowed to keep. That's great if you found something worthy and your conscience verifies it. But if it is unhealthy and you're being stubborn, you may fight for it and you may have it, you may cling to it and it is yours, you may never let it go, even up unto your dying day, but it may not be the thing you'll want to be found holding.

On the positive side, it can enhance your image to use a good habit to get things accomplished without excessive effort. Examples of good habits include: using a napkin or handkerchief to maintenance your mouth, driving safely and predictably so others can do the same by your example, practicing manners and courtesies, being of service to someone in need, and keeping your commitments at work and home. When supporting a good habit, any weightlifter will tell you that muscles have memory and you must program them correctly. Then, repetition will give the required results. So it is with acquiring and practicing good habits.

Bad habits include: interrupting people when they are speaking, not waiting your turn for something, biting your nails, speaking with your mouth full, and getting something without earning it. Ridding yourself of a bad habit involves recognizing, through observation, active compulsion and feedback, that a bad habit is at work. The more you become aware of it and want it to stop, the less power it has over time, and it will eventually diminish if you allow it.

Dysfunctional habits include: Taking something within reach that doesn't belong to you, allowing children to run wild, arguing with people consistently, and not obeying the words *no* or *stop*. Dysfunctional habits can lead to tragedies for the practitioner and those they practice on. Jails, hospitals and courtrooms are full of people who need help in stopping themselves. The key to the whole process is to become aware of yourself and what you are doing, and then determine if it's compatible in the home, business arena, or public places. Now here is where you come in, dear Reader. I couldn't possibly list all the good, bad or dysfunctional habits. So, start your own list and become aware of what you are, what you practice, and whether it should be a keeper in your belief systems, needs modification, or has to go by the wayside. Remember, it will be done to you as you believe.

As to becoming aware, you'll notice that all around you, at any given moment, there are things happening, both visibly and invisibly. It is impossible to key into and perceive everything that's occurring. We would go crazy if we had to, considering there are things in operation we are not equipped to monitor. However, within our little spheres of recognition, we have the ability to take in what is necessary and beneficial. This is accomplished by becoming an observer and receiver (of what you see and hear) as you navigate to and fro. The human body doesn't need to be told to breathe, blink, or keep the organs moist. It is designed to function automatically, then give feedback and input to you. You can be selective about increasing your personal growth through awareness, while at the same time becoming more attractive from within. Reading, conversing, keeping current on events and getting educated, all lead and feed personal growth. You control all this. One fun and amusing way to increase your personal awareness is to break some of your existing habits. Habits are hypnotic. They *train you in* to accept them. As I mentioned earlier, some are good, others are not. So what then? Learn to know *why* you do what you do. To practice this, become aware of what you're doing, then do the opposite. Going toward that which you resist doing will bring growth, and the resistance presents itself clearly, and is easily recognized. Just like rubbing your hands together in cold weather will stimulate blood flow, the following techniques will stimulate your personal awareness and decrease your hypnotic programming.

Women, try switching the arm you typically carry your purse on, and see what happens. You will be surprised what comes out of you when you do. I don't want to spoil it for you, so get your own experience and be prepared to meet your personal programming. Try putting your watch on the other wrist, and again, an entirely different set of sensations kicks in. For the bold, stop wearing a watch altogether. Try a different shampoo, deodorant or toothpaste, and change your routine when applying. Brush your teeth with the opposite hand. This one is hilarious, awkward and messy, but worth it. After some time, you'll end up stimulating the other side of your brain...fascinating. If you're typically quiet...speak. If you usually go first...go last. It is endless. Try fixing your hair differently. Women, there is power in this. It introduces you, and others, to another side of yourself. Eat with the opposite hand. This is like learning to eat for the first time, and has too many benefits to list. At first you will encounter resistance, so watch the suggestions your mind comes up with. The impulse to just switch back and eat with your usual hand will be strong. Resist it as you watch. Slowly, you will bring yourself to a higher coordination level. Your reflexes and your thinking will change with your eating protocol as your brain and muscles begin receiving new instructions. Try doing things you normally don't do. If you listen to a lot of music, cut it down, and if you don't listen to music at all, start it up. I highly recommend karaoke, either in front of a mirror, in the shower, or while driving a car. This has nothing to do with whether or not you're good at singing out loud. You're good enough to howl out a hit song and then laugh, which is the whole point. Throw out everything in your closet, around the house or in your car, that you do not use. Not only is this symbolic to an *inward* emptying out, but you have unconsciously tracked and remembered these items in your brain. Why do that? Use that freed up space and energy elsewhere. You will see a part of yourself that you've kept hidden, but is in there. I actually had to clean out my closet several times (I couldn't decide what to keep and what not to), until I did the mother of all cleaning. Each time I experienced torment over whether to throw something away, so I gave it the time test. My closet is so clean and organized, that now I couldn't tell you what used to be in there. I am free of it. In reference to throwing anything out, please be ready for the crazy, invisible and annoying rule that no doubt came from another planet, which says: *as soon as you throw it away, you'll need it*. Watch this one...it's not true, but will try to convince you otherwise. Good luck!

Another awareness jolt is to feel the pain of hunger. The brain will send a message that it's time to eat, as it normally does. Try ignoring the first broadcast. Watch how it keeps coming up. Continue watching, and you'll soon realize that the urge will eventually pass again. It is appropriate to remember that people can go without food for days, and that during emergencies and productive pursuits, often experience no hunger at all. Stand it for as long as you can, then eat as a favor to your body, rather than by command or compulsion. It is very rewarding to discover the principle of *eating to live versus living to eat*.

All of this will be very uncomfortable at first, but as you continue, using your common sense as you go, you will begin to free yourself of your programming. Your confidence level will increase because everything within you was originally set up to be controlled by your spirit and guided by the Holy Spirit, or breath of God. As you activate and feed this dormant part within you, you'll be stirring its ancient memory, and it will begin to awaken. The original system, or the way you were created (not born), is a magnificent state of being, designed to navigate through eternity, and when not receiving from God, to observe and enjoy. It is an existence that cannot be explained using words, without diluting the experience. You can get glimpses of it here on earth by practicing meditation disciplines and learning to be still. This involves the ability to quiet your mind and become an observer of your own thoughts. Your intellect was never meant to be the *go-to* source, but is just a maintenance mechanism that was promoted when mankind fell from grace. Come out from under its leadership, programming, suggestions, and selfish desires, and discover the mystery of creation, beginning with yourself. I want to wake you up from the inside so you can have a deeper existence here and now. You will find your own uniqueness and discover who you really are, and not what your circumstances or your environment are dictating to you. Bear in mind that we were created to commune with God in a way similar to the child-parent relationship. Learn about the child in you, where it went, what it is doing, and why it is not living the *child* role anymore. For the teens here, that won't be too hard. For those that have taken life so seriously because of setbacks, disappointments or the unexpected, you may have to lose the resentment and get over the shock, and in some cases the deception, before the full child activation is allowed to take place within you. Allowing the child in you to make decisions and come out to play under your adult supervision is one of the most satisfying experiences a mature person can have.

Girl Pearl: We are shaped, molded, and fashioned by what we love. So, take one part his love and one part your love...shake and serve!

To Party or Not to Party?

Where's the party? The party is within you, and you are the life of the party. If you want to add to that, go right ahead. But first, let's make sure you are secure, feel good about yourself, that you're able to enjoy and appreciate the little things, and that less goes a long way with you. When you feel secure enough to know yourself, then you are becoming ready to take your party out there to join others. If you do this the other way around, you'll miss the opportunity to experience *you* and to let others experience the real you at these gatherings. You merely become one of the herd.

Now, if you are planning on going out there, perhaps we should review a few things. First, be wary of parties in general, and inquire with your inner parts as to why you are there. Try even skipping a few, which will help you realize that one party is about the same as another, and basically, everyone there preys on everyone else. Taking a few steps back allows you to see more clearly, both the environment of it and your motives, not to mention that *you* are now dictating your terms to it, and not the reverse. It is good to do all things in moderation. A lot of time spent in the partying arena can *dumb you down* and diminish your realness and true purpose.

Never put yourself in a position of compromise, or where you feel awkward and cannot exert your true self. Partying can have that effect on some. You must maintain control over yourself and your surroundings at all times. Never accept a drink from someone else. I am sorry to say there are drugs out there that make you sleepy, dull, ineffective, and even paralyzed, and they can go into a drink very easily, as they are odorless and tasteless. Never leave a drink unattended, and if there is anything you don't feel right about, go with that feeling no matter who says what, even if it means refusing a drink someone has handed you. Women have good intuition, and if they listen to it, they will fare very well. Do not get drunk or even tipsy. Drink to be social, and stay in control at all times.

If you are enjoying life on its terms, where a little wine with your dinner or a beer at the old BBQ is acceptable, then this section may not be for you. If you are taking prescription medication for the right reasons, you might skip this chapter as well. However, using drugs and alcohol in excess, or for the wrong reasons, is detrimental. Anyone who needs drink or drugs to be motivated, feel good, live life, or go into action, is missing the purpose of life altogether. Aren't our daily encounters enough to supply stimuli and awaken our extraordinary lives? They are if you are living correctly. When you catch the flow of life and realize there is so much to do in so little time, your life has begun. Why, then, would anyone sedate themselves during this magnificent journey? It may be because the real mechanism, or the proper inner tool, is disconnected or incapacitated. It is not available because there is something in your life or your past that you're in denial about. You have been cut off from your inner parts and your life compass. Rather than wait to listen and obey your conscience so it can show you the way out, you have created a way with drugs, partying and alcohol. So, either you are not handling life properly, or you're carrying baggage from the early years. Whichever it is, you are being robbed of a fulfilling *now* life, and drugs and drink have locked you into your past and present pain, as well as into a cycle of doubt and confusion.

There are people who have discovered a shortcut, a way to command life or reduce it so they can live it on their own terms, neglecting responsibility and accountability. Excessive partying supports that mindset, and some have compromised their character and dignity by letting this empty lifestyle dictate to them. It begins with the simple, seemingly harmless (so you think) procedure of learning how to manipulate yourself either to feel good or not feel *anything*, using alcohol and drugs as a stand-in for the quick-life-fix. I have seen people drink to unwind, and an entirely different person comes out. I have seen alcohol bring out rage, self-deprecating humor, indifference, repressed feelings, painful memories and thoughts, past sins and embarrassing or inappropriate behavior of many kinds. To be sure, it will bring out what is in you, and for that purpose alone, it can be used to show you the depravity of your condition, which at some point, must be confronted. Something unholy has taken the place of the holy, that is, your inner parts.

To the sober person, the conduct that comes about from drug and alcohol use is neither cute, entertaining, funny, or relevant. It is heartbreaking. It is the outward demonstration of one who is empty inside. I often wonder where that conduct goes to hide in a person during the sober hours of the day. All of this (whatever comes out) is on the inside of that person, has been carried around all day, and is then released by alcohol or drugs, which relieves them of it temporarily. You see, none of that should be inside you. You are carrying around a heavy burden which interferes with your daily personal and professional obligations.

A good first step is to acknowledge that you are out of order and control. You are not functioning properly, though you may not know exactly why. Pause, or just stop whatever it is you are doing. Stop going out every night, talking on the phone all day, or eating when you are not hungry. Whatever it is, stop it. In addition to the physical pause, learn to quiet your mind and stop going from one thought to another. Simple meditation techniques, or the popular *working with your hands* method, can help you focus and stay in the moment. This quiets the mind effectively, because by being still you are not engaging it, or it is occupied with whatever task is at hand in the moment. You will notice that when you learn to quiet or apply discipline to your thoughts and behavior, your emotions will become manageable too. Second, don't *add* to what you already know. Many thoughts, emotions, or memories of past behaviors or traumas, will come to the surface once you start the fine art of being still. When they present themselves for your consideration, just observe them without adding or taking away from them. What is meaningful can be addressed, and what pulls on you which is *not* productive, if you do not engage or activate it, will pass in due time. Third, ask questions and seek answers from all sources until you make progress. Your childhood and your parents are a good place to start. Trauma took place in all of us during the growing up years. There was a time when our innocence was lost or injured, and the shock or

34

trauma of it has locked us into that moment. This is universal, and we all survived it, but subsequently, a piece of the real person was left behind. That void, or reminder, needs the right attention to correct itself, so we can begin to live normal lives, free of the resentments and traumas of the past. As adults, we can go back, taking our inner child with us under our protection, and seek, knock and ask questions, then free the child as we undo, correct and close any issues or traumas we picked up. Drugs and excessive drinking puts off the procedure, creates new problems, and keeps us from exposing all of what has been locked up in our hearts. Remember the rule: whatever you get into, gets into you. Let that sink in. It applies to the good and the not so good. It applies to everything. How you act, and the responsibility for it, is entirely yours as an individual. Remember, God does not desire the masses...he desires you! I want you to be well, do great things, and be loved for who you really are. If you fail to act by hiding yourself from a situation using drugs and alcohol, you bring down the responsibility solely upon yourself as an individual with a conscience.

Girl Pearl: Hide from anything you like except love. Oh, be found by it and bound to it; be not absent this day without it.

Willfulness

Enter into the world of faith, the world of believing without seeing. *How* we go about getting what we want in life is very important. You may prevail in everything you do, and gain all you want by being forceful, shrewd, uncompromising and insisting on your own way, and you are allowed to do so, but the price you pay will be steep. You see, God wants you to have the desires of your heart in such a way that compliments you and a new heart is created within you. When you go about your way without adhering to, and consulting your own conscience, you are cut off from God's purpose, and *your* purpose goes to work. It subtly changes you into an identity other than what God intends. The fine line between your will and God's will is just this: do everything you're supposed to do without becoming willful about it. Frustration, depression and resentment are all signs of being willful. They also create false feelings of loneliness and anxiety. Go anywhere you want without ambition, tunnel vision or stubbornness. Again, your will at work. Stop trying to have *your* way all the time and become aware that there are many ways, so be open to all of them. The right way will stand out to you and beckon you toward it. The wrong way will appeal to you like a drug, and will lack charity (love).

In due time for some things, and in the moment for others, you will be shown what to do if you remain objective, and without hidden motives. Have little or no agenda except wanting to do the right thing. There is no higher calling than this. The Bible defines it as righteousness, and hungering and thirsting for it defines you, making you very attractive to God and mankind.

It is not wise to have everything you want at any cost, unless you want to become vain, selfish, and insensitive in the process. Remember that the soul of a person stands in the middle of two worlds: the spiritual and the material. The one to which you respond controls you. The portion in life God wants you to have far exceeds anything you can imagine, and it will come to you...it cannot go to anyone else. When you try to create your own instead of waiting for the true one, your portion goes unclaimed and the false reward of the material world is substituted in its place. This is why we remain hungry after eating, and must keep drinking to satisfy our thirst for material things. They can neither quench nor satisfy like God's good gifts.

Realize there is enough for everyone. A heart of charity desires others to receive their rewards in the same way it longs to receive its own. This is an excellent first step toward less of your will and more of God's will in your life. Stop the insanity that comes from you, is kept alive by you, and is distracting you from becoming a child of God. Be anxious for nothing.

Girl Pearl: One woman reads another's character without the tedious trouble of deciphering. - Ben Jonson

Navigating Through Different Personalities

Okay, so you're going to meet someone for the first time. Keep in mind you meet people all day long, and therefore you're already spontaneous with this. What to expect? Let's have some discussion. Everywhere we go, two things will stand out. One, there are people everywhere and two, there we are, with them. I have noticed when meeting people or passing by them, more often than not, correct interaction is compromised. I once asked someone what their biggest challenge in life was, to which they responded: *navigating through different personalities*. At the time, I didn't think too much of this, but it stayed with me. As I traveled on and got more exposure to people, this statement came back to me. I was now finding it a challenge. Have you ever walked into a room and were ignored? How about when you are with someone, and another person comes along and begins talking with your friend, completely ignoring you? How about not even being acknowledged wherever you are, be it in a restaurant, retail store or by a neighbor, friend or relative? How about in a business meeting where introductions were made and you were left out? Not only do I not like it, but I will not do it to others.

Many times I've passed people who are staring down at the floor. This is not a natural posture. It takes effort to do that. Sometimes people withdraw into themselves, and by doing so, cut themselves off from the world. When you do this and get good at it, all of life's promises and all your treasures, waiting there to be discovered by you, go on hold because you are not available. Why do that? We are trying to improve ourselves and

37

upgrade our experience, not dilute or dismiss it. The very minimum we can do when passing someone on the street, in a hallway, with other people, on the way to the car, entering a room or in a church, is give eye contact and smile. Adding to it by speaking, is optional. Gestures such as thumbs up, the okay sign or prayer hands are good, and a nod or tilt of the head, or a slight bow are signs of friendly acknowledgment. Audible greetings invite reciprocity, and more profitable conversation may ensue. Statements like: *nice weather we're having; elevator's out of order; traffic jam; pretty hat!; where's a good place to eat?*...all help to break barriers between people. It's amazing how even the hardest looking exterior of a person will soften and respond when a little effort is made. Be that person who makes the first move, and you will see the results for yourself. There is also *the glance*, then looking away afterward, and glancing again. The second glance is optional, and you may want to reserve this one for those to whom you wish to send a message. You will also run into people who qualify for a hug, and then, of course, there is the old and familiar handshake. If you choose this one, there is a sub-communication in it you should know about. There are many types of handshakes, including the firm, the loose, the fingers only, the half hand, full hand, or long and short shakes, to name a few, each conveying the degree of enthusiasm, warmth, formality, moderation or restraint you want to project in varying situations. Learn by practicing on people to find your best approach.

In everything you do, and wherever you go, there are opportunities to grow and prosper, both personally and professionally. Navigating through every personality presented to us becomes fascinating and challenging as our awareness increases and we begin to participate. People Navigation 101 should be included as a compulsory educational subject. Why aren't we making it more mandatory than Algebra 1? For the rest of your life, you'll be interacting with people wherever you go. Why not get good at it from an early age? To be able to interact in a positive way with others is a skill designed to profit you all your life. Liking a person or not has little to do with it, as long as you don't hate anyone, because hate disqualifies you from the learning process. Learning to like someone takes time and even then, it is a personal choice. Discovering how to tolerate, get along, and respect other points of view enhances *you*, as you learn to listen without judgment. Also, you can benefit from people who are difficult for you to like, because they can teach you a lot about yourself. Have you considered you may see in that person something which reminds you of what you don't like about yourself? Perhaps the reason you can so easily identify a trait in someone else is because that same trait is in you! This is referred to as the *mirror* principle, where you see yourself (good and bad) in others. Use what you see in others to take stock of yourself. It may be painful to admit, since you won't always like what you see, but that's all the more reason to go *toward* what you see and expose it rather than dismiss it. Next time you see a tall, majestic tree, remember it not only took the elements…the strong winds, the cold, the rain and sun to produce what you are looking at, but it also took resistance to insects, fungi, and other plants and animals, for the tree to survive and flourish. In other words, *adversity* brought about its magnificence.

As you navigate through different personalities, if you can find the humor, stay focused, and don't take anything too seriously, then the world becomes your playground. I use the word *humor* because it adapts well to nearly all situations, and draws out a predictable response from others. It also tends to invite the child in you to participate more, and kids just know how to maximize the moment and have fun doing it. Your reward for navigating correctly through different personalities is in the memories, plucked like flowers from the fields of people you have met and touched, of the very moments you are navigating through. Study up on this subject and make it important to do so.

The first validation of a human being goes back to Adam recognizing Eve, and what his reaction must have been. I marvel that we look for life on other planets, but can actually ignore life here on earth by passing each other as though we don't exist. Sincere interest and curiosity in others is a form of practicing honesty, first with yourself and then with others. All of us, as human beings, have been given this inward interest in each other, but how often we suppress it and look the other way! Nay! You must go toward that which is natural to you, even when it seems difficult. Allow this curiosity to come out with interest and acknowledgment when one of your like-kind enters into your sensory range. The more you do this, the more you will discover the beauty of it, as well as the beauty within you waiting to be revealed. It brings good things out of you.

Girl Pearl: *The Universe awaits your next choice.*

Points of View...and Spiders?

When the wise old spider, who is able to crawl on the floor, walls, or ceiling, was asked for an opinion, she stated: *it depends on how you look at it.* We do well to remember the spider's point(s) of view, and be sensitive on how many different perceptions there are to any given subject. Getting stuck on "one way" which is usually *your* way, won't continue working for you, and will eventually backfire or, at the very least, make for a trying day for everyone else and you. Not only that, but you miss out on getting to know someone else intimately by failing to see things through their eyes.

In discussion about any subject, when a myriad of perspectives are at play, spider sense helps with our communications, and enables us to stay centered and focused while allowing us to see and hear another's point of reality. Being aware of the feelings and viewpoints of others produces a conducive atmosphere to move situations along toward resolution and results.

When dating, discussing, or exploring anything with anyone, use spider sense liberally. Try *listening* from the speaker's point of view rather than your own, and not only will you understand more about the speaker, you will become a better listener and a more attractive, inviting and understanding audience. Your growth awaits, and many will benefit from your example.

Girl Pearl: Life is short, and we have never too much time for gladdening the hearts of those who are traveling the dark journey with us. Oh, be swift to love, make haste to be kind, and be generous about it.

Hygiene Means Keep Clean

We should, at all times, be at optimum on the subject of hygiene. Your hair, nails, breath, teeth, body odor, and all the rest, should be presented at their best. Included in your makeup bag is everything needed to maintenance and keep your fresh, clean appearance current and up-to-date. Your clothes must be clean and you should always project an appearance of well-being. Cleanliness does that. You may be poor, but if you are clean, poor is not what will be remembered about you.

Consider that while you may be looking for someone to date, they will definitely be looking for you too, even when you least expect it! So, your default position on this subject should be high. You don't want to miss any opportunities! Keep in mind that the mixing of aromas from your deodorant, perfume, soap, and shampoo can work against you as the combination of fragrances overwhelms or takes on an unknown chemistry.

Girl Pearl: What is lighter than the wind? A feather. What is lighter than a feather? Fire. What lighter than a fire? A woman. What lighter than a woman? Nothing. - Harleian

Smell Good or Smell...?

As for perfumes, it is very important that you look and sniff into this. Not everything that smells good on others or looks good in the bottle, is necessarily good for you. A fragrance must be tried and tested to see how it interacts with your own personal chemistry. Also, others discern our scents differently than we do ourselves. What you think smells great may not transfer well to others. Not everyone will like what you like, and after all, this subject is about you and interacting with others. Testing at department stores or trying a variety of free samples to apply at different times, asking questions, and experimenting with this subject will bring about good results. After applying different scents, ask for feedback from people you trust. Remember, the wrong fragrance can work against you. Sweet or powerful aromas can drive people away, and actually work as a repellant. You want to compliment your own scent without covering it up altogether.

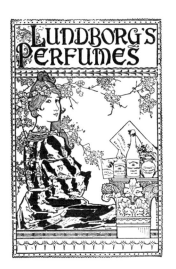

*Girl Pearl: If the heart of a man is depressed with cares,
The mist is dispelled when a woman appears. - Gay*

Girl Pearl: *Learn to separate the flies from the bees. Then, ordinary bees from extraordinary bees. Then, when you are sure, let your inner flower open to share your special pollen.*

43

None the Worse for Handbag or Purse

It is my humble opinion that a woman should always carry a purse or handbag of some sort. As you're well aware, there are some things you should have access to at all times: Change purse, cosmetics, identification, keys, brush, mirror, perfume, deodorant, gum or mints, sanitary applications and something very important and overlooked, tissues. Girls, tissues bring out your feminine side, are lady-like, promote etiquette, and are functional. Your personal stock goes up with the use of them, and if you'd like your stock to be further heightened, let me tell you that *hankies* are not just for the older ladies! They're prettier than tissues, they're floral, feminine, and won't be scratchy on your delicate noses like most tissues.

As for purses, you may want to carry one for style, function, or both! As one gets older and relies more on the purse of choice, compartments and sizes begin to make sense. When a man sees that a girl can go into her purse with a purpose, he takes note. It looks good, and says there is more to this woman than meets the eye.

Choose something that speaks for you. Alligator says one thing, fur says another. Just make sure you are aware it's part of your presentation. Leather and crocodile last longer than suede and fabric. The leather should be firm and buttery to the squeeze so it doesn't crack or change color. Any hardware attached to the purse will stress it out, so check for quality. Look for one with metal or plastic feet on the bottom too. Be sure to try the bag and view yourself in a mirror, as you don't want it too large or too small for your frame. Expensive bags can be a good long-term investment. Colors to compliment the clothes or the mood are always a hit, and there are times when just a small purse is appropriate. This can be carried by hand or light shoulder strap. On other occasions, you may need the larger model. Have fun with this. As a precautionary measure, pay extra attention before setting your handbag on the floors or counters of bathrooms, restaurants, kitchens, and even the floor of your car. Purse bottoms get filthy and may need to be cleaned.

Girl Pearl: *Win her and wear her if you can. She is the most delightful of God's creatures, heaven's best gift, man's joy and pride in prosperity, man's support and comforter in affliction.*
- Shelly

You are the Jewel in Jewelry

The wearing of jewelry is an interesting subject to look into, as it will give you insights about yourself. Women and girls get to wear jewelry. What a lovely and exciting world to take part in! These little pieces of emphasis are used to bring out your personality and compliment your image, or identity. I have seen some really gaudy, overdone, mixed-matched arrays of trinkets that if they could speak would say: *hey, will someone notice me, talk with me, and love me please?* A more alluring message to send would be: *hey, look over here! I like myself and want to be liked. If interested, why not come over and comment?* From there, girls, it is up to you to take it wherever you want it to go. The rule of never getting a second chance to make a first impression is at work, as is the concept of *less is more*. I did once see an exception, where a woman with a perfectly round head and accented facial features wore the biggest hoop earrings I ever saw. It was a clever presentation of herself, and worked beautifully for her. I have seen similar displays on others which had the opposite effect, of detracting from their appearances by adding too much. Your shape, features and personality must be taken into consideration for the optimum display of the appropriate jewelry, and shopping for these accents may take considerable time.

Different jewelry brings out different parts of you for all occasions: mild, wild, and elegant, to name a few. There is so much to explore here. Taste, application and how well you know what compliments you should rule the day. Do men notice these things? You bet. But these trinkets and details should all point to the main subject matter, the grand prize, and that would be *you.* It is you, girls of all ages, who control the experience. You, in effect, become Public Relations Managers, promoting a very important client. Your client is no less than yourself. Promote your best self.

Girl Pearl:
Where is the man who has the power and skill
To stem the torrent of a woman's will?
For if she will, she will, you may depend on't;
And if she won't, she won't, so there's an end on't.

- *from the Pillar Erected on the Mount in the Dane John Field*

Wake up Your Makeup

Makeup defined: *to change from one form to another.* Over the centuries, women used burnt matches to darken their eyes, berries to stain their lips, and young boys' urine to fade their freckles. They even swallowed ox blood in misguided attempts to improve their complexions. I understand what they were trying to do, but keep in mind that *less is more,* and to accent what you already have is what makeup should be about. Remember, the woman makes the cosmetics, the cosmetics do not make the woman. Too much applied, and Halloween is upon you, with vamp coming in a close second. Now girls, I have always believed that makeup was unnecessary. I am able to look at a woman and appreciate who she is, whatever I see. From my own perspective, beauty is defined by the whole experience (inner and outer) and not a check-off list. When the beauty of the inside lines up with the outer appearance, the experience can be very pleasant to the observer, the giver, and the receiver. Even God takes note.

46

What are some of the reasons women wear makeup? Perhaps it can be used to accent or highlight a feature you think worthy, but why? Am I wrong in thinking women believe if they *do not* wear makeup, they cannot compete with those who do? Why do some women put on so much? What are they saying and speaking here? What's the message? Do they know they are doing it? Is it worth the time and trouble to do all this? What is the return on time and effort invested? Do women tell other women if their makeup is not right? Did you know there was a time when prostitutes were called painted ladies? Doesn't that *imply* that what they *apply* is inappropriate?

In food, travel, conversation and people, accepting the natural "package" is the primary concern and *not* how to wrap it up nicely. Think of the natural beauty of nature, sunsets, ocean views, and landscapes, and then add to the list a woman...one of the most beautiful natural experiences around, a living and necessary asset to the planet. In the professional and corporate circles, I do not see glamour as an effective tool. While it garners attention, just what kind of attention it attracts is worth noting. Could it be a distraction? Is it a substitute for the real thing? Women were not put here to be used, but appreciated for their multiple talents. Using too much makeup detracts from that.

My parting thought is simply this: the woman is the prize. At the end of the day, that is what it all comes down to. If a woman is comfortable and accepting of herself, others have no choice but to join her. The opposite is true too. If a woman thinks she is not good enough as she is, she will attract those men who agree with her, then will plot to use, rather than respect her.

A real woman makes the clothes, jewelry, hairstyle and shoes all mean something. Without her inncr guiding light shining brightly, the elegant lady within will always come in second to the advertised, made-up person on the outside. I'd like to remind everyone that before makeup was, women were. They were here first, and were more than good enough. The application of cosmetics may accent what you already have and bring out some of your hidden qualities, but true beauty is still, and will always be, found within.

Manicures, Pedicures & You're the Cure

Women…girls…you really get to have fun with this subject. A woman who takes time to present her best self on the subject of fingernails and toenails is making good use of her available tools and skills. When your nails are presented to the world, it says a lot to both women and men. Men like a woman who takes care of herself. Properly done nails send that message. Now for those just starting out and still chewing gum, wild colors that make no sense to others, but look good to you, are not the way to go. Bubble gum and dark gothic may be pleasing to yourself, but not in demand by your suitors. If that is where you're at right now, have fun and enjoy. Perhaps having fun with these in private is something to consider. To the more advanced user of nail polishes, this is not an issue. By now, you know what looks good and shows good. Some of you even have the ability to look good in multiple colors that you can switch off to reflect your moods or messages. Good for you. They should be more pleasing to you, and when *you* light up, so will the one looking your way. You know what works for you, and it is you who must put it to work. Remember, these things are only little bread crumbs that point the way to the main loaf…YOU. You are the prize. Imagine some lucky man out there who will have the benefit, reward, and pleasure of your devoted company.

Put Your Clothes On

Women's clothing is an interesting topic. The clothes a woman wears will tell you much about the woman wearing them. The clothes were made for you, and not you for the clothes. Therefore, it is you who will make the clothes stand out when you wear a smart outfit. If you want to go around advertising for Victoria's Secret, you will attract men who want that secret and nothing else, and you lose in the end. Girls and women who reveal too much are sending the message they are not good enough, and need to add to their worth. They are saying: *look what you get first and then you get me*. Ladies, that's how it will be if you continue advertising that way. In most cases, it is how you start out which dictates how you will end up, and in truth, you want exactly the opposite of that. You want to be loved for who you are first, and the rest is a bonus for that lucky guy. My point is to be aware of the messages you are sending, and why you are sending them. Question yourself and your motives on this subject, and be aware of what you will attract by revealing yourself in suggestive and over-alluring ways.

The woman who dresses to enhance her natural style and personality becomes very attractive without having to put herself on display. A woman's flare, fashion, passion and personality should shine forth from within her like a beacon, and her clothes are meant to compliment the entire experience. Have fun working on presenting yourself to the world, but be ever mindful not to turn yourself into an outward display before you have first cleaned up your inner parts and begun to learn just who you are on the inside. Then, adorning the outside takes on more meaning. Allow the men in your life to love and appreciate *you* first, and then notice and compliment your outward appearance. During the Oscars, I observed how many of the pretty women relied heavily on their clothing to make their statements. Yet those who have done the work on their inner glows first, can wear *anything* on top of that and become a natural hit. You can put out a quality message from your inner parts, then compliment that aura with details that project your personal style with finesse...whether your style be vogue, chic, subtle, artistic, elegant, professional, demure, or outgoing and bursting with life.

Girl Pearl: *Put some glow in what you know....*
define, design, align, then shine!

Don't Wait to Lose Weight

Bodily weight condition bothers all who battle with it, and with women it may tend to take on a more serious tone. If you hate this subject, then it is for you. Sorry about this, but we need to talk about it. After all, ladies, I know you want to look your best, and presenting yourself that way will help bring in optimum results. Please let me go on record for stating that your inner well-being is the most important aspect of the weight issue. If all is well with you there, then whatever weight you are is not relevant or important. However, there are those of us that may need some discipline here, because we don't want food to be a substitute for what we're truly seeking. As with anything, your motives, and how you approach any subject, will determine the results or lack of results that follow. Everything we do must be for the right reasons. Having right on your side is like having God in your corner, and the opposite is also true.

There is no mystery about how to lose weight. Here it is, simple and true: eat less and exercise. That's it. No pills, no fasting, dieting, purging or trick meals. Finding the right combination of what your body requires, is the key. Your body's intake needs consist of three things: carbohydrates, proteins, and fats. Each of us has different requirements for each item, so you'll need to do your own experimenting to find what's right for you, and it's not hard to figure out. Mine is protein, fat, then carbo. That is the order of what I should consume from most to least. This balancing of the big three must be done for every meal. Also, eating several small meals throughout the day has many benefits. First, your stomach shrinks. Second, you have dealt with the hunger message. Third, your metabolism is kept at a higher rate. Lastly, you will not overeat when you practice this. Eat until the message to stop eating kicks in. Never eat past that. Eat only when you are hungry, and not out of boredom or when you mentally decide that it is time. Also, eat slowly so the message to stop will come, and you'll eat less.

Did you know that food can cause you to forget God or be a substitute for him, and even give you sensations of love?

People get lost in their eating habits, not realizing that their deepest inner parts are hungry, and they are feeding that craving with what may nourish the body, but ignores the spirit. How often have you found yourself standing in front of the refrigerator right after eating? What are you looking for if you just ate? It is an indication that something is missing, but what you haven't realized, is that food will not satisfy what is missing. Truly, you are hungry for something because you have a void, but you are seeking to fill it the wrong way. You keep trying to feed the void so it will stop pestering you. You find out through trial and error that it doesn't go away, and then you eat again and again to get rid of it. When someone is out of their flow, or not in tune with themselves or their environment, they tend to compensate for that disorder in a myriad of ways, without ever facing the real issue. Eating is one of the easiest things to do for the wrong reasons, and doing so may keep you from your rewards, your potential and your destiny. It becomes a form of slowing you down. Why? Consider that eating is fun and very satisfying in the moment. Comfort foods such as macaroni and cheese, mashed potatoes, or even potato chips, make us feel good. Eating can even help us forget our problems. Try staying in the moment next time you eat, and watch how your mind begins to wander.

Eating has become a universal quick fix to what troubles us unconsciously. We all know chicken soup can cure anything. Heck, good Chinese food, a rack of ribs and a good burger and fries can suspend all your troubles. It can have the effect of a sedative, making you dull and complacent to what is happening. The overly full feeling when you are stuffed says you used food to find an answer…too much food! The goal is to become aware of eating properly, so you don't gain unnecessary weight, and you lose the stored up weight you don't need. The end result is that you'll feel lighter and will get more done in more ways than one. This natural feeling is priceless. You'll have energy that can be used for more meaningful things like dating, waiting and making yourself into the person you want to be. When a problem or challenge presents itself, you are ready to fire back and resolve the issue. In times of stress and uncertainty, the world will come against you through your mind and emotions, and eating can provide a temporary comfort and escape. Then, when you have recovered from your episode or disappointment, you've got additional poundage to remind you of the mishap. Wrong choices produce guilt, so in addition to the extra pounds, you have guilt to contend with. The problem starts to take on a life of its own, and can become a vicious cycle. Compound guilt can become very high maintenance and lead to depression. We must reverse this process, and the first step is to become aware of your eating and *why* you're eating. Don't be willful about changing it. Go slowly and experiment until you find how to feed yourself correctly. Don't overreact, but take conscious control of what goes into your mouth and why.

Here are a few tricks to counter the *feed me* messages sent by the brain. Drinking water before eating (and when thirsty) promotes a full feeling. Chewing gum also fools the brain into believing that food is in the mouth and on its way, thus reducing the brain's signals to eat. Also, snacking to satisfy the message to eat makes the message go away. Of course choose a healthy snack. Eat slowly and chew well. Lastly, when eating carbohydrates, the body is slow or even reluctant to turn off the "I am full" message and will allow you to keep eating well beyond your needs. Your body is programmed to store fat and stay ahead of its needs and requirements, and performs that task automatically. *We* must control it. That is why the famous commercial featuring the man stating you cannot eat just one potato chip, was correct. The body supports it as a pleasure, so it can store up for leaner times. We don't need food to be as much a pleasure as a function, nor do we need to store extra, as there is food available wherever you go. Even rewarding children with food sets them up to be motivated by eating rather than accomplishing. The same applies to you. Eat what is good for your body, not good for your ego, which has a way of controlling and rewarding you. Ice Cream, second helpings of anything, chocolate milk, candied apples, donuts, pastries, fats, sweets, all feed the ego first, then you. We end up starving...for true life. You can treat yourself to certain goodies from time to time, but do it for the right reasons, be aware that you are doing it, and do not make a habit of it. When you do overeat, burn it off by exercising to offset it.

Food shouldn't be the focus of our every day lives. Do you remember ever skipping a meal because you were so busy either having fun or working hard? How about during an emergency…there is no craving for food, just action. Keep in mind you can go without food for 45 days or longer. All I am saying is that reducing your intake will not kill you, but make you more aware, so find the right reason to eat. Put eating in its place and seek a greater reward. Don't let it steal life from you. Learn to eat to live properly and not live to eat incorrectly. It takes time and discipline but is doable and reward-able to the inner portion rather than the outer portion of a human being. Remember, you can always eat, but losing excess pounds is a difficult chore. Eat less, live more, and find the balance. You never see overweight farmers, pioneers, or people in their nineties. This is something worth looking into.

Girl Pearl: You only get one life, but if you live it correctly, it's all you need. So it is with finding a true love. One will do it.

Girl Pearl: Your dreams are as infinite and as beautiful as the garden you plant them in.

Girl Pearl: Do not put off running toward, grasping, or experiencing your pain. Your growth awaits.

III. IDENTITY

Who Are You...Really?

Life is not complicated unless you are studying it, at which point you see how complicated it can become. But if you are *living* life rather than studying it, it's simple and makes perfect sense. Life is a gift, it's the best gift there is, and a gift that is meant to be used and shared. Just look around this planet. Life makes the earth stand up on its legs. We can always find a job, or something to do, but is that all you really want? Just to fill in the blank spaces and kill time? Or, is there something inside you, maybe it is clear, maybe it is not, but it is there, gnawing and stirring and wanting to surface? If that is the case, then you've got some work to do, and be glad for it.

I knew a man who, at first glance, I could see was authoritative, results oriented, and responsible. As I got to know him, I learned that he was also kind, caring, and a worthy man to know. What I learned from him, is that he saw the first part in himself, but was not aware of the second part. He couldn't see it. Imagine the joy he experienced when he discovered the special combination of skills, talents, and "being" inside him. Remember, it was there all along, but he couldn't see it. So it is with you. Yours is there too, waiting to be discovered.

Many who attend college have no clue as to why they are there or what they want to do while they're there. So everyone takes a business course and hopes to get a good job. Some even take the advice of others, who tell them what they should be doing, and do that instead. Yet what they need to find is their *bliss* or happiness. Let that trickle down from the brain, pause at the tongue, and then roll off into your mouth. Taste it before you swallow it. *AAAH BLISS.* Whatever makes you happy, content, at peace, full of wonder, holds your attention, has you coming back willingly and gladly of your own accord, appeals to you moment to moment, while feeding and guiding you from within, is *bliss food*. Find that, and you have found everything else. Thank Joseph Campbell for all the work he has done in this field, and for summing it up in three words: *follow your bliss.* I love the way it sounds. When you find it, you may end up driving a bus, plumbing, working with your hands, studying foreign languages, helping school children, doing legal work, exploring the medical profession, or bringing to pass great plans for society in whatever city you live. Strangely enough, success, contentment, and satisfaction follow with no effort, and you'll be living the life that was given to you and approved. You have lined yourself up with your destiny.

Welcome to the world of me, myself, and I, or better known as *you.* It is your exclusive world, where you can custom create an environment that attracts your desired results. So, I ask: *who are you?* You see, you came into the world fresh, pure, innocent, with a clean heart and blank slate, unspoiled territory ready to be imprinted. So, who had their first shot at you? Your parents, or an equal authority figure. They were the first to lay out the course for you to follow, be it right, wrong, or indifferent. Although it may have been with the best intentions, an unnatural course and a false destiny were, nevertheless, set before you and have entered into you. You also got some good in there with the *not* so good, but the result is that you are not your true self. This is the fate we were all given, and is a universal fate, lest you think I'm talking only to you.

Your false identity is unrefined, has been thrown into a hostile environment, and will seek out nurturing, coaching, nudging, guiding, and counseling to make itself stronger, while all the time becoming wronger. It is in opposition to the destiny God intended. Consider also that your parents started out the same way, as did their parents, and their parents, going all the way back to our ancestors who choked on the forbidden fruit. My point is that we do not have our own identities, but the ones imprinted on us by those who raised us. Therefore, we must begin the process of emptying out. This statement implies that we are full of the wrong stuff. The "how to empty out" is the part that's missing. Yearn to be set free without activating your will. Long for, seek and desire the truth, good or bad, but the truth at all costs. Your sincere desire will be honored.

The first truth is the most cherished....that is, the truth about yourself: who you *are*, and who you *are not*, which now begs the questions: *just who am I? Do I even know? Can I know? How can I be sure I know?*

The point is illustrated beautifully in the story of Tarzan. It's the story of a little boy who has been abandoned in the jungle, and raised successfully by a race of giant apes. As he grows up, of course, he mimics the apes in all they do, and knows no other way. When he reaches a mature age, he begins to notice subtle differences between himself and the apes. They are hairy, grunt a lot, are different in color, covered with hair, they walk with difficulty, and actually look entirely different. One day he sees himself in the reflection of a pool, and it all makes sense. He is not an ape. Okay. So now he knows who he is *not*. But that doesn't tell him who he *is*. So it is with mankind. We were raised with core beliefs, ways, ideas, perspectives and thoughts which were not originally ours. So who are we? We do not know, but to ask is the beginning of finding out. Thus we begin the journey of finding out who we are (and who we are not), and why. Are we really who we thought we were all this time, or have we been acting out someone else's programming? When Adam was first created, living by just existing was all he had to do. He had no desire to discover who he was or where he came from, because he was in fellowship with his Creator, and was also egoless. But all of this has changed for everyone born after Adam. Now, we must seek to find out who we are, why we are, where we are, and why we're here. This is creation versus birth.

Everyone begins the discovery of *"who am I?"* at different points in life. Typically, this is not the all consuming question of those in their younger years. Although you cannot avoid discovering about yourself as you go, it may not be your immediate and active goal. Until it becomes a real question for you, the most you can do is expose yourself to as much as possible to encourage inner growth and stimulus. As you get older, the subject of identity begins to emerge, and when it does, it doesn't go away. Why? It is the beginning of searching the heart for the very essence of your being, and of knowing where you came from, where you are going, why you are here and what is required of you. We are seeking our origin, which will lead to the *now*, which will lead to the *forever*. Knowing your purpose, your contribution, and the part you play while visiting here, is what you are here to discover. You are part heaven and part earth. It is the heavenly, or spiritual part that gives life. This has reversed itself in you, and must be righted within you in order for you to come around right again.

Some of you, for one reason or another were not appreciated growing up. That being the case, seeking others' approval for who you are and what you do has become your way to gain acceptance. This is not the way to go about building your confidence levels or to learn about yourself. In fact, it is high maintenance for yourself and others. *You* must know your true values, and when you recognize them, it doesn't matter what others think. Trees with strong barks and trunks have encountered harsh weather, storms and excessive sunlight. Thus, we have the Redwoods...a direct product of cause and effect. You are searching for your personal causes and effects, your beliefs, fears, thoughts, ideas, whether your own or programmed into you, which created your current (and past) positions. When you discover the truth about yourself, it will begin to transform you from the inside, along with your thinking, into another type of creature. Journey well to discover these truths...they will speak to you. Trust yourself and the One in you to verify.

I have often watched birds going about their routines, and there is absolutely no confusion or doubt in their daily comings and goings. They know what they're doing and why, and just go about doing it. You may also have observed this with ants. Scouting ants go out alone over all the terrain searching for the common good. When they find it, they secrete a chemical trail from the find all the way back to the nest. They report the find, and the nest now moves with a purpose to retrieve it. You see the same procedures in bees gathering pollen for honey production, and in birds flying with the seasons. These lesser forms of life function beautifully, know what to do, and our observation of them should compel us to question ourselves. It is not necessary for us to understand *why* they do it in order to get the proper lesson; the lesson for us is that they *know* what to do, and we do not! This should cause us to stop and ask, *"What should I be doing?"* How sad it is to see a complex and higher form of life operating at minimum, and how exciting and fulfilling to see that same form of life functioning at optimum. We send out messages about ourselves all day long, wherever we go, which must line up with our hearts and minds if they are to be effective. When the messages we send are in conflict with who we truly are, confusion abounds. For instance, the woman who dresses and acts provocatively, may be crying out for love, but is sending out messages for sex instead. This mixed message isn't lining up with what is in her heart, and therefore her true motive is not interpreted correctly by others. People are not always what they appear to be, beginning with ourselves. If we do not know who we are, how would anyone else? Perhaps others are responding to who we think we are instead of who we really are. This is rampant in the dating and marriage circuit, and is costly to all who engage, which is why it's important to seek out and discover your identity first. Make it an adventure motivated by love and a sincere desire to know. If done correctly, you will meet up with humility and this will lead to many beneficial experiences.

Until you begin the journey of learning who you are and who you're not, you will always sense something missing. Well, that something *is* missing and to find what it is and fulfill it, is part of God's plan for you. There is a void in you that cannot be filled with anything other than God's realness and purpose. He put it there intentionally to cause you to inquire. As you search for this purpose, be careful not to go on tangents, or substitute *anything* for the realness you are seeking. Substitutes are just that...distractions from the *real,* or *reality.* Everything you are, or want to be, is already inside you waiting to be discovered. You must peel away the outer layers, just as you would an onion. Each layer is relevant to the one before and after it, and has something to give before it reveals the next layer; then, in the center of it all, is a very sweet and pure core of innocence that is bursting with flavor, life forces, mystery, and origin. So it is with you. It may take years, or even a lifetime to unravel, so discover it with patience. As you travel through the stressful and unfulfilling *I want it now* generation, go with patience, knowing that all you are to know will be revealed, if your motives are pure and good. Until you have breakthrough on this subject, it is permissible to search out and admire role models, and emulate those virtues in them that are admirable, noble and worthy. In the private world and wherever you go, there are fine, upstanding women from all walks of life who have found inner value and performed well.

As for purpose, until you know *what it is*, and this may take years, begin the discovery process by eliminating what you know it *isn't*, or as I prefer to say it, *what it ain't*. Observe, learn, and become aware of all the *what it ain'ts* in your life. As an example and starting place, you don't rob banks, plan to lie, cheat, or steal or inflict intentional harm on people. You already know you are none of those things. You will discover many things that *ain't it* for you as you journey, which will begin to clear the way for those things that *are*. Become aware of what you are drawn to, and what you aren't, and let yourself gravitate toward what you know to be right, true, good and virtuous. Standing up for these principles is what makes you *you*, so they must never be compromised. There are times and situations in which it will be extremely difficult to act on what you believe, but then, that is the real test. In doing so, you will, at the same time, be gravitating away from all the *what it ain'ts* as the purification process continues. Learn about yourself and begin to establish your own boundaries. There are many sources of self-help, and all add a modicum of their truths to yours. Glean from many sources, and receive what is appealing and attractive, and reject what is not to your liking. Spend as much time as you can on this subject through observation, feedback, staying aware, and listening to input from others, to add to your own personal life experiences.

Having once found the key which unlocks who and what you are, you must never let it go, or surrender it to anything or anyone. Until then, to seek, knock, ask, journey, inquire, and investigate, are not just requests, they are instructions to be carried out. When you do this, you'll find purpose, fulfillment, satisfaction and many other rewards that come from just *being* who you are as you travel through your life adventure. This is well worth pursuing and discovering, and the beginning of this transformation is quite simple. No fanfare, no thunder and lightning, no burning candles, rituals, rehearsing, scripture-quoting, moaning, tongues, lining up of the moon and stars, incense, incantations, or anything that comes from you or anyone else. Deep down inside a person, something holy and eternal signals to the everlasting, and takes you with it as it was meant to be. God the Father, the Holy Spirit and the Christ are enough, and that's just about how simple it is.

Girl Pearl: Go toward, even run toward, any truth about yourself, however horrifying, which may reveal to you your true condition.

Be Do Have...It All

Be who you are. **Do** what comes from being who you are. **Have** the fruit of that behavior. ***Be Do Have***. Be wary of using the formula in any other sequence. ***Have Do Be***, for instance, is the person who thinks that in order to *be* somebody (a false identity at work), to *have* is the way to go, so she goes about the *do* of that, to create her *be*. She buys jewelry, clothes and an expensive car (have); she gets a feeling of wellness from it by dressing up and driving around (do); and creates for herself a false being (be). Then, ***Do Be Have*** is the person who thinks that to *do* will lead to her *be* and then she will *have*. This one becomes a people pleaser, an enabler (do), and indeed may win approval of others, creating a sense of false identity (be) that brings acceptance or love (have).

All these formulas work in various orders, but only the ***Be Do Have*** produces the desired results every time. Applying it in all you do will result in developing the true *you*. The alternate formulas produce results that lead you to willfulness and a false life, though with extreme subtlety. It's like having a car that runs, but is not finely tuned. Every time you start it up and drive around, you're reminded it isn't quite right, and it will remain that way until you initiate repairs. If you want to run at optimum, ignoring the *Be Do Have* is not an option. Go with your flow, which is your correct posture from *being* who you really are. Learn what that is. This will include admitting your faults and errors, and having a closer look at your blindside. You must learn to become honest with yourself, slow down, and become cognizant of what comes out of you, and why. Keep what you like and throw out the rest. Reference the Repentance chapter as necessary. Then, your errors will begin to dissolve and a welcomed change will come your way from living the *Be Do and Have* (in that order).

Girl Pearl: *Love is so delicate a flower that praise tends to make it blossom, while discouragement often nips it at the bud.*

The Real You is Enough

Ladies, we all have our different attributes working for us. You may be cute, sweet, gentle or pretty, have a nice shape and walk; you may be articulate, innocent, and have attractive facial features, or perhaps you just present yourself well. Be aware that these work all the time without you having to call obvious attention to them. If you add to them by over-emphasis, exaggeration or boasting, immediately the realness disappears, honesty and truth are belittled, the original beauty is diminished, and meaningless chatter abounds. Everyone is falsely enthralled for the wrong reasons, and phony rewards are exchanged. You will feel false attention, receive praise, and the person who acknowledges it feels good because they validate it for you, whether they believe it or not. Two wrongs trying to make a right with all their might will not take flight and succeed. All this is unnecessary when you are being real and being yourself. The real you is sufficient, and does not need to be added to or interfered with. Your body shape, hairstyle, and positive features all work without your permission, and adding to them or calling notice to what is already working, will detract from the real you and open you up to a false existence comparable to eating sand: filling, but not nourishing.

Try very hard not to be someone else. You see, dear girls, everyone else is taken, and there is only one you. God's point of view on this subject must be very important indeed if he went to all the trouble to create *the one and only you.* You may be tempted to act like someone else, especially if you see that person receiving a lot of attention. You think if you imitate what they do, you'll get that attention as well. But in doing so, you're practicing to be someone other than yourself, so whatever attention you may get will not be real. Don't compromise on this subject. The question *"who are you?,* is a worthy question to ask and seek to have answered. It takes time to find out, and it's time well spent. Actually, just being aware of the question as you journey is enough to begin the discovery. You may find you'll have to spend some time unlearning before you can begin to discover your likes and dislikes, but you will have an adventure in the process. Your life becomes like a motion picture, starring yourself, with no two movies alike...AMAZING! Equally amazing, is that as you become aware of who you are, you have a say-so as to how your motion picture develops and progresses!

Now, let's go over this from another point of view. As mentioned earlier, at some point in your early life, your innocence was taken from you (more than once) in one way or another, and something else was substituted in its place. This is universal, and applies to every human being. Discover how this happened, mourn over it, and want the change that will be presented as you inquire. To start the inquiry, pause or stop your present conduct and methods, whatever they are. Take a time-out. Then, having something meaningful to do at the same time will allow you to reflect and meditate. Working with your hands is highly recommended. Sitting still quietly and staying in the moment is another. The point is to stay out of your thoughts, which are similar to a logjam in your mind and soul, and let them come and go freely while you *observe* them. Picture yourself watching a parade passing by. Something in the parade will catch your attention and draw you into it. Become aware of that, and let it go. It will pass as you return to watching the parade. So it is with thoughts. They can pull you in if you let them. Learn to watch them and not react to everything that pops into your mind. Begin to see yourself as an *observer* of yourself, if you will. At some point, things that have been buried within will start to un-jam and come to the surface. Incidents, behaviors, wrongs, rights, traumas, fears....many things will surface for correction, review, repentance, forgiveness, or to be just plain thrown out. Then, let the child in you bloom under the supervision of the new adult.

When you begin to do the inner work of becoming a woman of value and claiming your rich heritage as a unique person, others cannot help but notice and inquire. Do not be tempted to create another false image as this happens. There is great effort involved in keeping it up, and the reward you expect to get from it never pans out. If you are going to take on the inner work required to progress, do it sincerely and with pure motives. If not, you will just find yourself doing it over again, never discovering your true self, while valuable journey-time has been wasted. Remember the rule: *if you don't take the time to do something right, you must have the time to do it over again.* Journey-time or lifetime cannot be manipulated, replaced, or extended. In fact, there are no guarantees in life as to another precious moment, let alone another tomorrow. Please make your moment and all that you do in it count for something, so you will have no regrets, now or later, and you will experience a fuller life. At some point, you will come to realize the potent lesson that life teaches which is simply this: quality of life is preferred, and quantity comes second. Start practicing this now. No shortcuts for you. Enjoy and appreciate every moment and be glad for everything. In the doing of this, the heart of a child is preserved within you. Very attractive quality to have. Very easy to love, too.

Girl Pearl: Until the woman makes her outward beauty have inner meaning, it is but a show. To make it true, she must herself be true.

Never Give Up

Whatever it is you are looking for or desire, must be pursued with vigor, and as a quest that never ends, until you find what you're after. Nothing must come between you and the desire within you. But remember, you've got to work for it, and it is as simple as just doing your part. In most cases, the pride and ego must be worn down and pooped out in order to access the truths within us. This is not easy to do, and, in fact, may be one of the most difficult endeavors a person will ever undertake. It is seldom accomplished without the help of an honest and true friend or mentor, and one who is very strong. This person of trust will stand for your rights and help to break you of your wrongs, but you must allow it, want it, and your motive must be to get well.

When two people come together and open their hearts to each other, anything can be accomplished. People who are threatening or uninviting make the process even harder. Thus, they need a stronger person to stand up to them if they are to have a breakthrough into and unto themselves. If you can find such a friend, hold fast and let the adventure begin, knowing that it will not be without suffering and pain, but a worthy and noble adventure it shall be, one which must never end until you get your answers, whether it takes several years or all your life. Who knows when or where your insights will come, but if you're longing and desiring to acquire your mystery in the right way, for the right reasons and with righteous motives, just remember there are laws that say you'll find whatever it is you're seeking. So throughout every phase of your life, during pre-dating, dating, courtship and marriage, live with this credo in your heart.

Girl Pearl: *If you ask God for a true man, be prepared for him to make a true woman of you….and it may be painful.*

Quiet Desperation

Henry David Thoreau coined one of the most poignant phrases I have ever come across to describe mankind's condition:

> *"Most men lead lives of quiet desperation and go to the grave with the song still in them."*

We owe this man a debt of gratitude for summing up in a single phrase, the condition of mankind's continuing propensity toward living unfulfilled lives. *Quiet and desperate* are not our callings, yet how often we readily choose them. Our minds and emotions will take us down that road, but our hearts beckon us another way, and it is the heart we must follow. The heart must win, and win it will, if we allow it to. Your emotions cause you to doubt and distort, oh, but your heart, dear Reader…your heart, if allowed to pursue its desires, will lead you to places you cannot imagine…places where all your answers reside, all your desires are found, and where your purpose opens up before you like a scroll. It will lead you to where *quiet desperation* has no meaning and occupies no space. The kingdom of God is within you and is very accessible.

The state of "quiet desperation" is the result of not mining your own gold, or the gold in others. Un-mined gold does no one any good, but lays hidden and undiscovered beneath the surface of the earth. Yet, it is there, was always there, and unless one goes after it, will remain there untouched. So it is with truth, and the pursuit of what is in your heart. It is well worth delving beneath the surface to seek, discover and bring forth. Obstacles will come your way to interrupt, redirect or stop you; opportunities and offers to accept less will present themselves to you continually; diversions, decoys, digressions and delays will all conspire against your pursuit, but do not let them derail you. Instead, take all of what comes against you as a sign that you are on the right track.

Why settle for a quiet, desperate life, hidden secretly inside the darkest parts of your being, feeding you despair and lack of purpose? It is contrary to why and how God made you. Open up, come out, inquire and seek truth. If you have something to say, say it. If not, go your way. If you break that rule, then you are being driven by unsavory sources. Once you give in to those voices, you are captive, and the holy place in you has been invaded and occupied. If you have something to do, do it. If not, be still. Go about your business; live your life and let the Holy Spirit, through your conscience, guide you. It is time to go inside to journey. You have journeyed enough on the outside. Learn about yourself and see how marvelously you are made. Apologize to no one as you seek out your answers and find the truths that will set you free. It is very doable, so please don't give up on a very important subject...*you.* Remember, the woman who seeks nothing or accepts less than her portion, gets what she wants too.

Girl Pearl: *When seeking virtue, do not give up principles for any gain that will take possession of you.*

INstruction from WithIN

Intuition, or instruction from within, is what we are looking for in life's journey. It's the personalized navigation system of your inner parts which came into the world with you. Each one of us gets this individual service for life, and it requires only that you activate it by listening and obeying the still, small voice within you. It is not to be found in your mind, but in your conscience, and you do well to learn to recognize it and desire to hear from it. It will never leave or forsake you; it is closer than a brother; it cares for, and is committed to you, and works closely with your own common sense. It is discovered and activated while in the practice and pursuit of all your issues of life. As you address any issue or begin any project, remain aware as to what you're doing and how you're doing it, leaving room for common sense to show you something extremely important. What you are looking for is *your* correct way of doing things. I am not referring to selfish, robotic or stubborn ways, no, not at all. I am speaking of the *insight* you are given as you proceed into a situation. This insight is specific to the receiver and sent by the One who knows what you need, and what he wants you to see and learn. It defines your identity, or *who you are*. Become aware of the false call or "cattle call" and resist the temptation to surrender and go along with it. That is the wide road. Shallow answers have no depth, whereas depth offers no shallow answers. No two people are alike, nor are they in the same place at the same time. Why, then, do we try to hide in conformity? Even though we are all similar, we are far from being the same. Discovering how this inward instruction works in you is the most important journey you will ever explore, and will lead to many other rewarding adventures. There is another way and it is a very familiar way indeed. It's called *your unique way*, and it's the narrow road, custom designed for you.

This inward instructor, your spirit, is your true leader, not your flesh, mind or emotions, which must first be disengaged for your spirit to go to work naturally. It does not need your help. When you decrease the input and reliance on your mind and emotions, your "know" begins to give you glimpses and insights on where you came from, where you are, and what is expected of you. It is all very pleasant and user friendly. The unseen Spirit will guide and educate you in all things that are relevant first to you, and only you, and then everything else, in time. This is where you will discover your personal relationship with your Creator. It all comes from within you, from the world of wordless words. Imagine a beautiful sunset that appears and you are overwhelmed in a pleasant way about the experience. Now, try explaining or writing about it. It is diluted and cheapened. You cannot take what was revealed to you in the wordless state and put it into words without suffering a loss. We actually dumb ourselves down by trying to do so. All the clichés are correct. Let go and let God; find the inner you; seek the child within...but the "how" belongs only to God. The devil, the world and your own flesh will be quick to instruct you and fill the voids, thus keeping you from feeling the pain that will awaken you from within.

Girl Pearl: *No man knows what the wife of his bosom is, no man knows what a ministering angel she is, until he has gone with her through the fiery trials of this world.* - *Irving*

Suffer for the Right Reasons

Be ready to welcome adversity and hardship, for when you do, these two friends in disguise will help define and create your character. At the very least, do not fear them. Consider how the wind makes the trunks of trees stronger, how the little seed has to burst out of a shell in order to grow, and how the supposed death of a caterpillar leads to life extraordinary. Consider the uncomfortable pressure put on coal to form diamonds and the worthless piece of sand that eventually converts to a beautiful pearl. How much more, then, will the beauty in you be enhanced when suffering brings it to the surface and goes full cycle in you? These are all examples of suffering for the right reasons, and will reward you in the end. Patience and the willingness to finish what you started is all that is required to get up and get going. Look forward to adversity for it is bringing value in disguise.

Many of us face challenging obstacles that we didn't see coming, and that appear overwhelming, yet it is these very mountains which are opportunities for new growth. We must never forget the answer to the question.....*is life good? Yes, it is!* Some of us worry, and think too far into the future. While it is wise to be aware of what's coming and its consequences, let us not forget to return to the moment where reality is awaiting us and the answers we need *now* are found. There are times when things look, sound, and feel quite bad. No doubt about it. This is the time to let go and lay down your will.

There is a point where a person has done all that can be done, and the rest is up to the powers that be. Remember the famous statement, *this too shall pass*. Boy, have I gotten a lot of mileage out of that one. Life is to be lived, not in your mind and emotions, but in the fullness of all you possess. Time is a precious commodity, as we cannot recapture what was spent unwisely in the world of time. If you are a mature individual, then you get to say: *I have made it this far. There were times when things looked bad, but somehow I made it. I will continue to make it whatever it takes.* If you are young and just starting out, behold how many others before you have prospered, learned, and have had their fair share of calamities, but are still here to encourage you. This is what life is made of, and what one person can do, another can do also. Look forward to your turn, as it is happening now.

Girl Pearl: If men would only understand when a woman says to just...hold her. Perhaps women can teach them more about this very important subject.

Are You Too Tough?

It doesn't make sense to see a woman acting tough. (Sorry, to all tough girls!) A woman's femininity is her most attractive, fascinating and captivating aspect. It has been given generously to the female species, and when actively engaged, enhances the subject (you) considerably. It is your *default* state, and when you stay in it, it will serve you and attract what is good for you. A word of caution...it will also attract what is bad for you, because males are attracted to innocence for their own

71

gain. When someone is trying to take advantage of you, *now* is the time for your masculine side to come out and protect you.

We do not want it to *stay* out, however, or become a normal part of your day-to-day existence. It is just a coping or surviving mechanism, and not a lifestyle. Many of you were taken advantage of when you were young and impressionable, you've had trauma, your tender heart has been injured more than once, and you've toughened up with the determination that you'll never allow yourself to be injured in that way again. Not only that, your defenses are activated, you swear you'll never trust again, you've hardened your heart against love and surrounded yourself with a wall of protection. Oh, and one more thing in case you didn't know: you are walking around with a very heavy load of unnecessary and unattractive baggage that goes by the name of *resentment*. Instead of trying to manipulate the

72

suffering to offset or minimize any shock in your life, realize the injustice of it, repent at the circumstances and the part you played, and then let it go. Always come back to your true self to start fresh and anew. What has happened, is that you are compensating for the trauma and pain you experienced, and the *real* you is prohibited from coming out. Your wound is showing, and you are not healing or recovering. This is because you have not responded correctly to what has happened to you. There is always risk involved in being vulnerable, so there is a modicum of truth in your feeling that it is unsafe to trust again. But there is also a way to handle it, dear one, that *doesn't* injure you. The real *you* deserves the real life experience, and there are forces in the world intent on robbing, interfering, and tricking you out of it. Let it be known that God has a system (a foundation) that prevents those forces from ever prevailing against you, and it's a sure thing. Protect yourself first and foremost, and please consider the following:

Relinquish the resentment you have for those who have injured you, and if necessary, any resentment for yourself. This may require time, patience and outpourings from your inner parts which will typically come forth with great pain, sorrow, weeping and suffering. In whatever ways it comes out, whether with words or no words, whether in sobbing, silence, stillness, tears or groaning, it will be understood by the One who knows you better than you know yourself, and hears the cries of his children continually. As you begin to heal and venture out again, remember that *trust* is something that is earned over time, and not to be given away quickly. Slow down and take all the time you need. As you become familiar with someone, you also become comfortable, and begin to relax and enjoy as you go. You slowly learn *who* to trust, who *not* to trust, and *how much* to trust. Learning to trust again, this time with the adult in you leading the child in you, is a vitally important part of both your journey and your recovery.

If you are a tough girl, you have already learned not to open and expose your entire heart to just anyone. Take all the time you need in proving the credibility and sincerity of someone before allowing yourself to become vulnerable, but when the time is right and the person is proven, you must begin to take small risks of openness again. Remember that trusting the wrong person too soon and without proofs may have been your mistake in the past. Your personal confidences should either not be shared at all, or reserved to share only with someone who has already passed your trustworthiness test. You will know who they are and how to proceed as you go. If no one exists for you right now, consider a diary. The point is to guard your inner sanctum and only share it with someone you trust entirely. Also, be prepared to develop a second skin, where you feel the pain, but move on, instead of letting it stop you.

Protect yourself responsibly when you have to, but do not stay in a permanent state of alert, or lock in your prior experiences through resentment. For those of you who have toughened up and remain in that condition, be still and reflect on the time or times you lost your innocence. You may think it is too painful to revisit, or that you cannot bear the suffering involved. But consider that you are already suffering the results of it every day, and may I add, that you are suffering in quiet desperation, all for the wrong reasons, and until you confront it, you will suffer the rest of your life. Go toward the pain and the reality of what happened, revisit it correctly, and you *will* suffer, but it will be for the right reasons, and will be short-term. It will begin the recovery and healing process which leads you back to becoming a whole person...vulnerable, trusting and dare I say *softened*, but oh, so much wiser than you were.

Girl Pearl: *Not all those who know their minds, know their hearts as well.*

Lark or Owl...Whoooo Yooou?

One day out of the blue, someone asked me the following: Are you a lark or an owl? I really didn't know the answer. I asked what it meant, and it was explained to me that a lark is at its best in the morning, and an owl at its best at night. Wanting the best of both worlds, and to prove how incredibly gifted I was, I ended up saying: *I am both.* I got through that moment, but something wasn't right. Looking back, I didn't really know myself, nor was I using this little jewel of a tool correctly. Now, I will share it with you to help you achieve your optimum. **Lark:** If you go to bed early and awaken early, you are a lark. **Owl:** If you go to bed late and awaken late, you are an owl. When I finally reflected on this and answered the question honestly, I discovered a hidden cache of energy that had always been there, but had never been uncovered. I found out I was a lark. Realizing this empowered me, and even changed the way I went about my daily business.

In day-to-day life, chores must be tackled, agendas must be carried out, plans must be implemented and work must get done. Not knowing how to maximize one's potential causes the process to be lacking, tedious, and more time and energy-consuming. When I discovered myself to be a *lark warrior,* and my optimum operation to be when I first greeted the day, I began to schedule all my heavy duty work projects for the mornings, channeling my natural, productive energy toward them during lark hours. Whatever problem confronted me could not prevail, nor could any weapon formed against me succeed, when the powers-to-be and I were all lined up in my preferred mode of morning action. There is nothing I cannot accomplish when all my energy is *lark on.* The opposite is true. I do not engage anything serious out of my lark mode. It just won't get my quality time and attention, so I schedule my daily activities accordingly.

Discover your mode...lark or owl. Money cannot buy this. It is free, and awakening it within yourself is all you need to do. Start by determining whether you function your best in the morning, noon or night, or combinations of the three. The inner harmony which comes from discovering this secret will compliment both your personal and professional life, because once your energy is focused accordingly, you can hit what you're aiming for with less effort. You'll be in your own personal flow, and nothing that needs to be addressed can escape your attention for long. You will get so good at optimizing your energies, that you may run out of things to do. This only enables you to take on more responsibilities, adding depth, purpose, growth, deep satisfaction and a sense of accomplishment to your inner self. Prior to understanding this *self*, feelings of dread, procrastination and even laziness can easily overtake and distract you because your own personal ducks are not lined up. Of course, there are some exceptions to the lark and owl rules. Emergencies, as they come up, must be dealt with regardless of the mode. It's *game on* when summoned. The body helps by supplying adrenaline and we must meet the crisis, come *lark* or *owl*.

Retraining yourself from your natural mode is possible, although it will never quite fit right. You can switch to either one, and may have to at times, but you'll never achieve mastery in making a full conversion to a bird that is not your true bird. Also, you cannot be both birds at a hundred percent optimum. Supplementing or manipulating the process using outside stimulus such as drugs, excess coffee or high energy drinks will throw off your equilibrium, and you risk becoming dependent on what you're ingesting instead of using your natural powers and energies.

In your natural mode, others will begin to notice that you get things done, and it looks good on you when you do, but no one has to know whether you're a lark or an owl unless you want to share it. What *you* will get out of it is a higher awareness of your surroundings and how you relate to them, and in time you will become more effective by using less energy. More of *you* will appear. May the force be freely with you on this one. Ladies, this is a force that can move mountains!

Girl Pearl: *Next to God we are indebted to women, first for life itself, and then for making it worth living.* - *Bethune*

Playing Hide & Go Seek...To Win

Remember playing hide and go seek? A most excellent adventure that costs nothing. The thrill of trying to find a hiding place while someone is counting down; the additional thrill of staying still and not attracting attention; finally, the seeker gives up and you have won the game, only you don't know it! You hid so well that no one could find you to tell you, and sometimes they even left without you. So it is with life. To hide, to hold things in, to go into yourself and not come back, is not a good journey for life. Let this not be confused with being shy and modest, which can cause one to be reserved, but not actively hiding. As long as you are aware of your shyness, in time you will find a way to deal with it and blossom. Remember, I am not suggesting that you become too vulnerable as you learn to open up. You must choose carefully who you become vulnerable to. However, even the flower must open up to receive sun, rain, wind, and entertain the bee, then, at other times it closes. If you're locked up inside yourself, you'll never experience life to its fullest, and people will never really get to know you...the real you, so you subject yourself to being continually misunderstood. The world inside you, yearning to be revealed, longing to be recognized, understood, and then flourish, remains stunted and dwarfed, resulting in a deep sense of worthlessness and low self-esteem. Tragically, you become accustomed to it and eventually accept it as your life, resigning yourself to less than the generous portion of your God-given share. In addition, this unnatural stress directs itself toward your inner parts and your organs, which can cause damage via various illnesses. Don't confuse this experience with your true destiny. There are many false lives, stemming from false beliefs. Some were handed down to you; some were force-fed to you, and others you picked up along the way. This isn't living, but merely existing and drifting through life without point or purpose. You must find your way out of yourself!

It is a high maintenance existence to hide in your mind and emotions. It can become addicting to the degree that it becomes your reality, and coming *out* of it becomes abnormal. Think of the diseases of ADD, Alzheimer's, or just plain forgetfulness, if not checked and corrected. Playing hide and go seek in your mind, means the real you will be hard to find. One of the common symptoms of this is to have discussions with yourself. It can manifest itself out loud where you are partaking in an imaginary discussion right out of your own mind, and actually answering a thought. People who are homeless and living on the street are often seen to be arguing with themselves. Perhaps they've created another world more to their liking than the real one. No one has been born into this.

There are many causes for someone to withdraw into a fantasy world or an alternate reality. Trauma, resentment, shock, survival techniques, and compensatory behavior are all tickets to the journey out of the normal realms. Then, fear, insecurity, and ignorance keep us there, in the dark of life. In that place, you will not find your true destiny or portion. Not knowing how to pursue it, you have learned to not be known or found, and in essence, you've hidden from life by withdrawing into yourself and creating another world. But you learn quickly that *that* sword cuts both ways. No one gets in, but you don't get out either. It is safe in that world, but oh, so lonely. It is time to unlearn and detach from the *hiding* role, and learn how to play the *seeking* role correctly. You risk getting hurt when you come out, so expect it to appear to get worse before it gets better. You will eventually transcend the system and find your true balance and existence. It is worth any risk to do so, considering we will not return this way again.

A very simple practice can be employed to lessen the occurrences of being in your mind. Once you become aware that your mind is wandering, realize it, and bring yourself back to the moment and to whatever task is before you. The more you practice this simple technique, the more you will find yourself living in the "now" which, by the way, is where God resides. Keep in mind that resistance to anything precedes personal growth. When you find yourself not willing to face or address something, realize this could be growth trying to enter your world. Go with the newness and welcome the change. Stay in the moment. Putting it off too many times leaves you behind in another place. Hey, life is happening out here, not in there.

Obsessing with your thoughts, ideas, and fantasies tends to make a welcoming place of refuge, but it is not a real place. Many of you won't remember the days before *call waiting* came into our homes. If someone was trying to get in touch with you over the phone and your line was constantly busy, it meant one of two things. First, it could be that the line was out of order; or second, someone was having one marathon of a conversation. It wasn't uncommon to ask the operator to check the line to see if it was working. Someone is trying to reach you and cannot get through. That is how solutions look at you when they are trying to come help you. They can't get through! You are either too busy to receive help, not available, or you are out of order. Be available, and receive what the days and the moments want so badly to bring you.

My dear girls and sweet ladies, come out...come out wherever you are, and *be found* living and sharing your life. The greatest gift you can leave behind is the gift of yourself...that people actually *knew* you and not only knew *of* you. Everything else remains less than that. Remember Thoreau's statement, how mankind leads lives of quiet desperation. This amounts to hiding from life, living only within our minds where it safe, but unrewarding. Some of us hide so well we develop fears along the way that never allow us to be found. The pain from this can be lonely and unbearable, yet people all over the earth are walking around in this condition. The second part of this famous quote reads "and go to their grave with the song still in them." Whew! Don't do this please. Whatever caused you to go inside and never return must be looked at, visited, and conquered. Life is to be lived and experienced, and your portion is out there waiting for you to claim it. No one else can have your share, so don't worry about theft, or that it does not exist. Not only does it exist, it belongs to you alone, and it is only you who can apprehend it.

Girl Pearl: *One must spend with the heart if they wish to purchase a good life. The mind gathers and stores knowledge, but it is the heart that spends it.*

79

God's Free Gift...The Moment

You must spend some quiet time "being still" with yourself, for the purpose of letting what is inside you come to the surface to be seen and sorted out. It's like cleaning out a drawer or closet, where you keep some things and throw others out, and new space is created in the process. In this way, you begin to find out and pin down who you really are, because this method begins to reveal who you are not. The clutter is being thrown out. The process is enhanced when you work with your hands, which has the added benefit of helping you stay in the moment. Listening to the inner direction is the first step, then the *why* and *how* will be revealed as you progress. Having knowledge of this moral compass is necessary, and using it is mandatory. It is to be obeyed.

Oftentimes, I see human beings traveling without the use of their inner compass. As they navigate through life, their joy of *being* is missing. The going to and fro is more important than what they see and experience while going. Their journey is in their minds, emotions and wills, instead of in reality and the moment. To come out of your mind and thinking, to leave your emotions in a neutral, manageable state, and to let your five senses just *experience*, or in essence, observe, is to completely put yourself at rest. This is your *default* state, it is the state you were created in and will return to, and the same state of receiving and observing which Adam was in before he fell. It is restful indeed. If you practice observation correctly, you will become a receiver of profitable input and data from the highest source, and many valuable truths pertaining to your journey will begin to surface and come to you from within. Past traumas, unresolved issues, sorrows, unanswered injustices, resentments, unfulfilled dreams, all that has been swallowed and is hiding within you, will be regurgitated in order to be sorted out and confronted. At some point during all this, new directions, corrections and suggestions for life will also be offered to you. Answers to questions and problems will come to you as you stay in the moment and allow them to do so. Resist the temptation to analyze. Don't add or take away from what you see or hear. Just observe.

Beneath your surface are buried treasures which are stored and protected by you. Some you are aware of, and others you are not. One of the ways to discover them is to engage people in conversation, dialogue and exploration of the subject matter until your inner treasure is sighted. It involves risking…the risking of yourself. It will surface with time and encouragement, and consists of meaning, depth, substance, and the truth that sets you free. When you find that truth in yourself, you can easily recognize it in others. Using the techniques of dialogue and stillness will bring forth untold insights, revelations and truths about yourself. Small talk doesn't do it, nor does common talk or repetition. Time and patience, along with an earnest desire to find what you are looking for, will produce good results. It is appropriate to mention that there are a lot of disciplines such as Yoga or meditations that can help you journey in this regard. Being still is a healthy and meaningful practice, and many incredible discoveries are waiting to be made once you begin.

Contrary to being still, is emotional living, which consists of highs and lows. Observing them as they come and go will eventually lead you to travel in a more even existence, with only minor twists and turns, mild ups and downs, and less roller-coastering. Nothing should have the ability to disturb you, but everything should compliment you. Traveling this way promotes inner peace and allows your true strengths to come out and do all the work. Desire more of these talents and skills, and less of you and your will. When you can stay in the moment and allow things to pass by and through you without engaging your emotions or thoughts, then you are on your way to becoming the real woman of God. Thoughts come from the lower nature. Let them go as they came. You are trying to diminish them and let the higher nature take over, which is knowing what to do in the moment. If it is not there, say and do nothing. Be still, which is putting to rest the fallen nature and letting God in you speak. Become aware of the *push and pull* of the distractions you engage by choosing to live in your emotions. The instant you realize you are overcome with thoughts and emotions, bring yourself back to the moment you are in, and whatever is at hand. Just watch and observe. There is no burden in the moment except that which you bring with you. Relax and see your shortcomings, including your pride, your will, and your constant striving to make, or not make, things happen. When you see them, if you do not interfere, you will experience a sorrow passing through and by you. You will also realize that it does not belong with you, and as you watch it, it goes away. Every new high creates a new low. In your quiet time you may find what is driving it, as well as what started it. In the end, the void that is created from it being discovered, then leaving, is full of suffering, and that suffering is a cry to God. Everyone must pass this way.

I remind people constantly of the rewards to be found in the moment. Whatever you are doing and wherever you are, built into that moment is your share of life in the *now*. *In the moment* is the ultimate payoff and place to be. Often I hear people make statements of regret based on hindsight and analysis.....this will never do. Here is an example of how the moment gets distorted and gets no respect: two people meet and start interacting together. The conversation is free-flowing and mutually satisfying. It goes back and forth, forth and back, and both people prosper in the moment. When they are done sharing, caring and dialoging, they prepare to go their own separate ways. Now here is my point, and what I want you to consider. It is simple in nature, but be cautioned that your mind can distort and play tricks with it if you allow it to. Before leaving each other, each party was asked if they shared everything they wanted to. Both replied *yes*. Then they were asked if there was anything else they wanted to discuss. Both said *no*. Next they were asked if they were holding back anything, to which they both replied *no*, they were not. Finally, they were asked if they accomplished all they wanted to at that time, in that moment, and to their satisfaction, and both replied *yes*. They parted ways. Now, fast forward an hour, a day, a month, a year or ten years. They meet again. One brings up that she wished she *would* have said and done more. The other says, I *should* have done the same. Both agree that more *could* have been done, and done better. Both begin telling each other things that they are now remembering. But the error they made, and the trick which was played on them and all of us, is this:

82

remember how they were asked in the moment before they parted ways, if their interaction was complete, and they both said *yes*? Hindsight, regret, and *shoulda coulda woulda,* being added to your thinking and thoughts later and after the fact, is not honoring the moment you were in. Reality has its own rewards. The moment is an innocent and effortless place (if you let it be), where things that are to be said and done, get said and done. The premise is that there are no accidents, therefore what was said or done in the moment was what was supposed to have happened. This is reality. This system was here before you were, and will remain after you leave. Learn about it and show it some respect. Moments cannot be modified, redefined, or recaptured. You must learn to receive them, observe them and keep moving because the next moment is in line waiting patiently and innocently to greet you. They come, then they're gone, off into eternity never to been seen again. Why are moments that way? They're like molecules, stars in the skies and grains of sand. They cannot be counted. They go through eternity from everlasting to everlasting. The answer is so simple it eludes most people. There's an endless, eternal supply of moments that never runs out or exhausts itself. On and on they go, *ad infinitum.* They are messengers of the life force used by the Creator, who invites you into the moment to participate in it with Him. God is the moment maker and he is very good at this. What does the moment require? Qualifications are to be aware, to practice honesty with attentiveness and responsibility, to optimize the experience in the moment you are given, and then learn to become a child of the *now.* If you have something to say, say it. If you have something to do, do it. If not, that moment is complete and you should journey into your next one. Don't live life backwards. (Live spelled backwards is evil.) Don't live life in your mind, live it in the moment. There is no regret in the moment, there is no *woulda coulda shoulda,* there is only what is meant to be there.

As you enter this journey, stay the course, be worthy, be an observer, practice stillness by quieting your mind and keeping an eye on your will and emotions, and the layers of a false identity will be revealed as they peel off. The light and the truth do the work. You do nothing but receive. The end result, whenever that is, will be a child left standing.

Girl Pearl: Maybe God wants us to meet a few wrong persons before meeting the right one so that when we meet the right one, we should know to be grateful for the gift!

Because the Universe Says So....That's Why

All dimensions of the Universe operate by principles of various forces, dynamics, and commands. These are not negotiable, and are mandatory to our success, survival, and existence. They continue to play their parts in a dependable way, and we benefit because they do. They rule and prevail, and we are invited into their realms as guests and observers. Wherever you go, their laws, procedures and applications are in effect. Take flying for instance. It is the stress applied to the soft wings of a bird via an air current that produces the lift. We imitated that principle when airplanes and space vehicles were designed. The force of one thing applied to another, under the right circumstances produces flight, or the ability to navigate away from the ground or earth for periods of time. So, the laws of the ground known as gravity are manipulated for a time and the laws of the air prevail. If these laws are not applied, flight does not take place. It is important to notice that the laws are doing their parts without fail; it is the human application of them that sometimes fails. When one applies the specified dynamics necessary to any field, one will prevail accordingly.

There are dynamics pertaining to life, dating and marriage, which operate in precisely the same way. When a person wants to have sex outside the marriage oath, then the honor, meaning, commitment and blessings one has longed for will not be called forth, and can never prevail. Just as universal laws pertaining to flight cannot be ignored if flight is to take place, so God's commandments, when applied or ignored, will draw forth the corresponding result. You can break all the commandments, and he will allow you to do so, but you will not receive the rewards, approval, or benefits that come from keeping them. What does it prosper a man to gain the whole world, but lose his soul? Immoral or less than acceptable behavior cannot be rewarded, nor can its consequences be avoided. You are absolutely free to choose any particular behavior, but the consequences that follow will not be yours to choose. They will come. You will reap what you sow. Therefore, honor the prompting of your conscience regarding your behavior, and let it have the final say on all subjects. As you do, you will be sowing seeds of righteousness into the invisible, intangible world, and you will reap a harvest that is deeply satisfying. The behavior you choose will determine what your harvest will be, just as the farmer who wants corn must sow seeds that bring forth corn. Once his seeds are in the ground, his harvest becomes invisible, but if he is faithful to his purpose, he will reap corn in due time. Now apply this rule of law to yourself. Pursue and sow seeds of honor, integrity, righteousness, kindness, virtue and good character, and your corresponding harvest, invisible but unavoidable, will not only be beautiful, but plenteous and attractive to others.

You cannot substitute anything for the real experience and expect to get realness in return. There are false or substitute joys and rewards, but be cautious not to confuse them with the real ones. A substitute may give you instant gratification, but no closure, satisfaction, or meaning, and your soul does not gain from the experience, which means that neither do you. Simply speaking, you want God in everything you do, not something imitating God and giving false rewards. Our needs are complex and require honest effort to achieve optimum results. Read the example of doing what you want and getting what you want *incorrectly* in the following chapter, *The Monkey's Paw.*

Girl Pearl: *Never apologize for showing feeling. When you do so, you apologize for the truth.*

The Monkey's Paw...Be Careful What You Ask For

The Monkey's Paw is one of the best known lessons available to teach us something about life, ourselves, good vs. evil, and shortcuts that appear to help us, but end up hurting us instead. Its message is: *be careful what you ask for, and from whom you are asking.* The theme comes from a horror story by W.W. Jacobs based on the premise that you can change your God-given destiny by interfering with your fate and attempting to create a new one, but only at an enormous cost which you cannot foresee. If you challenge life from the position of God, the monkey's paw will answer you for a price.

One version of the story tells of a man who was stranded on an island by shipwreck. He discovered a box, half buried in the sand, and in it an old, but intact severed paw of a monkey with an inscription on the wrist in small writing that said: *Speak to the paw, you shall be in awe. Three times given, you will be driven.* Now, instead of going about to discover what lay in store for him on the island and rising to that occasion, the man saw an opportunity to instantly improve his situation. He realized he had stumbled onto a type of magic which would grant him three wishes. He eagerly began the thought process for the first wish, picked up the monkey's paw, and said: *I want to be the richest man in the world, bar none.* Instantly, he was led to a large underground cave on the island, full of treasure without end. There were rubies, pearls, diamonds, emeralds, and gold and silver coins as far as the eye could see. He was elated, but quickly came to his senses when he realized that as long as he was stranded alone on the island, all his riches had no use and would do him no good. After thinking this over, he picked up the monkey's paw again, and said: *I want to be the richest man in the world, off this island and surrounded by people.* He instantly found himself surrounded by people, all calling him *sir* and *boss.* He was no longer on the island, but in a great underground cavern somewhere in the largest diamond mine ever discovered, of which he was owner. A cave-in had just occurred, and the richest man on the planet was surrounded by people with no way out. He paused and considered what had happened. He became instantly aware that he was dealing with a diabolical power…one that tricks and confuses whoever does business with it. He realized there would be no way to out-wish the monkey's paw, and the only way to win would be to have not wished in the first place. Knowing he had but one wish left, after careful consideration and deliberation, he picked up the monkey's paw and made his final wish: *I want to be back on the island without having found the monkey's paw.* Instantly he was right back where he left off, and with joy, went about to explore his new home and discover what God had in store for him by bringing him there. He began using his God-given gifts, and a new life unfolded, where he found his answers and correctly brought forth favor…both with God and himself.

Girls, let the moral of the story speak to you. Be leery of the wide road and the shortcuts which bring you instant answers, but false results, and rob you of the right way to your true treasure. You can be willful and choose your own road, but its consequences will not be yours to choose. Begin the work that was given to you right where you are. Do this correctly and you will bloom. Be cautious of the easy road where life's lessons are ignored and worldly gains are received at the expense of your fellow human beings. Instead, do what is fair, right, true, decent and honorable, and the rewards that follow from traveling this way will reach the depths of your soul, define your character, and transform you into a very attractive person. Turn away anything that resembles the monkey's paw…the easy, beguiling way, the dishonorable way. Learn to earn, then cultivate, what is rightfully yours.

Girl Pearl: When the gifts of a woman all line up and are brought into the moment, the universe sings a delightful song and all who hear it are better for it.

87

Your Word is Your Honor

Long before contracts came about, before anyone became complex, needy and wanting, there was the simplicity of just giving your word in the moment, whoever you were. This is a most satisfying existence for yourself and those around you. In this pure condition, it makes sense that whatever comes out of a person's mouth means something. Somehow, over time, this has been replaced with outward dynamics (written contracts) designed to help us get ahead in the world. In essence, the simple life experience has been diluted and cheapened. People are quick to further degrade the character and integrity dynamics, and sue each other in courts of law. The absence of righteousness in mankind leads us away from our true destinies, where laws must be in existence to guard against this fallen nature in man.

If the issues we argue about were to be taken up in the heart, and correctly implemented and shared, the human race, as a whole, would be complimented and enhanced. Differences can be quickly resolved and mitigated. Your word should mean something. I'm referring to the inner honesty, which is being true to what is right in your heart, and then sharing that right with others. When you say you are going to do something, the measure of your character is what you are really sharing when you do, or don't do what you said. It is a true measure of your worth and of who you are. If what is coming out of you is less than honest, disingenuous, tricky, deceiving, half-truth, confusing or has hidden motives, then correction and attention should be directed to you to clean this up right away. Your credibility as a human being in all situations, is predicated upon your honesty levels. You must choose a side and serve it.

All of us came into the world unspoiled, innocent, and full of wonder and awe. Along the way, something happened. We began learning the ways of others, and the ways of the world, and developed a system, or a series of outer beliefs to live by. Some of us strayed to the left or right and didn't come back, becoming casualties of temptation. The Devil and Daniel Webster (the story of a man who sells his soul, and a man who fights for him to keep it) proves that lying, cheating and stealing work. Think about this. They work because people wouldn't keep using them if they didn't. But what you don't find out until after you've used these systems and made their deals, is that you have paid an invisible price, and a high one, for their results. You begin to realize you've been robbed, and that you're missing something, but how it happened, what exactly is missing, and where and when it got lost, all remain a mystery. The process is subtle and works very slowly. You don't even realize it's happening until one day you sense the void and discover that your aura, or innocence, has been jeopardized. Your character has been injured, and your peace of mind, calmness, and day-to-day existence is compromised. You have shifted from one set of rules (God's) to another set of rules (prince of this world) and your new master is not a respecter of persons. In his world, you are considered worthless and to be used, disrespected, abused, then discarded. Because you have become a part of that world, you act and relate to others in like ways. Consequently, your only gain is the material reward for which you sold out. You have everything, yet in reality you have nothing.

Have you ever heard it said: *there is no rest for the wicked?* Haven't you seen decadence follow that which comes from attaining wealth the wrong way? I have seen drug dealers, swindlers, and thieves build palaces, buy expensive homes and gifts for others, and hold lavish parties, all stemming from attempting to purchase back something they lost when they made the dark bargain, namely their honesty, self-respect, and righteousness. They have gained all the world's goods, yet those goods do not satisfy, and the guilt associated with the wrongful gain will not allow them rest or peace. Thus a paradox. To all appearances they have everything, but inside they have nothing. Earn your way with honesty and integrity by choosing the right way, and be content at all times for what you have, and for whatever situation you are in.

It has been said that your character is what journeys on after you die. If that is true, invest in this wisely. The successful application of this dynamic promotes you as a human being, made in the image of God. You will become attractive to your like-kind, and to the One who sent you here. The lack of it has the opposite effect. The practicing of character on each other brings out the best and deepest parts of the human adventure. Tell the truth, the whole truth and nothing but the truth, and discover the world of 'yes,' 'no' and 'I don't know.' The freedom and simplicity offered in that world is most satisfying. Failure to address the honesty issue by not holding ourselves and others accountable, supports the degradation process further. We do not need more sin in the world. By not holding yourself accountable for what comes out of you, you risk attracting someone who has advanced themselves in unscrupulous ways and gains. Your wrong, and the wrong in that person will get together, and each will bring out, or nurture, the wrong in the other, leaving the more noble aspects in each other behind. Why would you want to devolve instead of evolve? Traveling toward the good is the journey. We want to narrow the road we are traveling on, not widen it, and this process is accomplished from moment to moment. Honesty is the way to go…and the *only* way to go at all times.

There is a remedy for lying: it is simply to *stop* lying, and the truth will go to work right away. You may feel a slight discomfort, embarrassment or even a small inner pain as the dynamics of the two worlds shift, and you practice more of one and less of the other. It is like going through a withdrawal. Don't interfere with this process. Just observe and experience it, and it will pass. It is a cleansing of your inner parts. You are realigning yourself with the good…that's all. Begin this now, also keeping in mind that the little white lie does not spare you either. It needs to be fed and joined by other white lies, and becomes bigger and more complex, until the father of all lies is upon you and in your nature. It is the same with taking something that doesn't belong to you. A piece of gum, a pen or paper from your boss, even loose change, if not yours, will cost you more than what their combined value is, times a hundred. Consider for a moment even something of as little value as a penny…one that does not belong to you. If you should take it, surely no great loss will be suffered by anyone else. It is what the penny represents. It can exist in two dimensions. One where you earned it, and it is yours to use and command; the other where it earned you, and uses and commands you. The realms of dark forces and righteousness are both trying to join you. Dark forces prefer you to have the penny incorrectly so they can join you; righteousness requires the right way to prevail before it joins you. When you choose the right way, it is sufficient, and all who participate in it are honored for their loyalty and devotion. Cheating another person has the same result. While you may have gotten away with it, the cheating or beguiling spirit got inside you and honors and respects your loyalty and devotion to its world by making you a cheat in expensive clothes or a nice car, with some extra cash in your pocket. Putting a facade on your sin won't help you. This is not acceptable to God or man.

When I've put in a full day's work, and in that day have handled all that came my way, and in the doing of it, sought what was fair, right, true, just and good, then I sit down to a meal. It may be as humble as rice and beans, or as grandiose as roast turkey with all the fixings, it doesn't matter. Whatever it is, it's sumptuous and satisfying. It is my reward for a good day's work, and gratifying unto my inner parts as well. After that, a good night's rest, then I am at it again. Money cannot buy this contentment, although it can offer one hell of a substitute. Still, there is a difference between the two that can be felt in your inner parts. One gives contentment the other unrest.

I have seen people at restaurants or Disneyland, who, at first glance, I knew had saved for weeks or months to have their outing. They were not well-off, and had saved and scrimped for the experience. They were grateful and happy to be where they were, and doing what they were doing. Even their walk was filled with gratitude and humility. They may not have ordered the most expensive items on the menu or at the park, but they treated themselves to a good time. At Disneyland, perhaps they were not able to buy souvenirs, extra treats or perks, but they went and saw the sights, and their rewards were perhaps even more meaningful than others, because they worked hard for it.

Honesty is still the best policy. You can take shortcuts through life, but it will be you who turns up short in the end.

Girl Pearl: The question is no longer what does a woman want, but where will she put it all...

Humility Rules

Humility is a very important virtue to nurture in yourself, and one you would hope to find in others. Have you ever witnessed someone going about their business, working hard, focused, and thankful in the act of what they are doing in such a way where it commanded you to affectionately stare or take a second look? People practicing humility can cause this reaction in others. Humility is defined as: *not proud; doing something out of the goodness of your heart, not for yourself; freedom from pride or arrogance; the act of being humble; and an absence of vanity.* Those practicing humility benefit deeply because their sense of purpose is engaged and being carried out through the practice of serving others. There are different states of humility, the highest being putting others' needs before your own, and the least being to serve without recognition or acknowledgment. *The least* may be interpreted in this world as of little or no value, but is interpreted differently and highly esteemed in another world. People who have, and practice humility are easy to approach and speak with, and others will always be affected by their presence.

I once managed a large, well-known unit of a major restaurant chain, where the owner would come in unannounced purely for the pleasure of visiting one of his many units. He would not call attention to himself, and instructed us to pay him no mind when he visited. He would come in on Saturday or Sunday mornings when we were the busiest, pick up two coffee pots and make rounds...which was to visit everyone seated and offer them coffee. No one knew who he was, and he so much enjoyed living and participating in his dream with humility and gratitude. I also once worked with a multi-millionaire who would race to answer the phones when they rang. All the employees would have to take the second and third calls. He loved talking with people who called, asking them questions and solving their problems. When people called in and insisted on talking with the boss, he would say "him speaking, how can I help you?" The humility of being available when others are not, is attractive and never forgotten. Another man I worked with who was very well-off, would visit his places of business and pick up trash from the parking lots and surrounding areas. He never said a word to anyone, but others followed his example. I once worked with a man who would clean up so thoroughly after working on a construction site, that after awhile I would start complaining about wanting to go home. "The place is clean enough" says, I. He'd reply, "we go home when we have cleaned up as though we were never here." We argued for weeks, then one day I gave in and learned a little bit about the secret to humility. Give yourself the gift of humility, then re-gift it to others.

Girl Pearl: In relinquishing the temptation of sex in the moment, you have chosen a side. What you did not know, is that in the very moment you took a stand for what you believed, in the invisible world, your true and intended love began making his way toward you.

Do Unto Others Works

You are a walking, talking advertisement. You're peddling your first impression wherever you go. Your presence is at work whether you know it or not. I want to emphasize courtesy and manners in all your interactions, whether in person or on the telephone. Nothing is more attractive than someone showing the proper respect and etiquette toward another human being in every situation. This opens doors widely. Do you recall seeing manners being practiced by children? It melts butter in a pan.

In this world we are constantly in the business of interacting with people, and the stakes are not merely social, but sometimes financial as well. Anytime you are dealing with the public, you get exposed to many mentalities, and navigating through them requires discipline and tools. What we like, and the way we like to be treated, others like too. To understand what works for others, start by looking to yourself, and you will have a wealth of data. It is safe to assume that what goes for you, works for everyone else. Treat others as you would like to be treated. Courtesy, respect, kindness, communication, patience, loyalty, honesty, commitment, steadfastness, professionalism, sensitivity, service, and truthfulness are all virtues you would hope to experience from others, therefore you must demonstrate them yourself. Keep in mind that whatever measure you use in your treatment of others will find its way back to you. How fortunate we are to be able to wake up each morning and look forward to practicing these virtues on others. This daily, hourly, minute-by-minute practice will help develop you into the person you want to become. Be glad and rejoice, when someone is rude or unkind to you, because you've just been presented with an opportunity to practice patience and kindness in return. *Do unto others* works very well, and the rewards of it, whether visible or not, will come to you in a myriad of ways.

The *do unto others* rule also applies to dating. Girls, ladies, women…do you like to be led on and teased by men, or manipulated by vagueness, ambiguities and mind games? Do you enjoy feeling trapped in a state of emotional sadness and confusion caused by conflicting messages, impure motives and cat and mouse chases? If you don't like this, don't do it! For those who do, I would not want to be in your shoes. You will pay a heavy price down the line, and gain little in return.

Girl Pearl: Man has his will, but woman has her way. - Holmes

Femininity: A Most Powerful Asset

The feminine power a woman possesses is something to behold. Wow. Let that sink in for just a moment. You have real power. Let that sink in too. Along with this power comes great responsibility and accountability to yourself and others. You must decide to use it for the good. When a woman lends this power to a man in the right way, the world takes notice and laws are activated which have been in effect since the beginning of the human race. Great things come into play and good things happen. The opposite is true too. Remember Helen of Troy, whose beauty and charm brought war to many countries? How about Delilah, who pedaled her goods to deceive and bring down Samson? And let's not forget Bathsheba, whose beauty tempted King David to the point that sin, compromise and judgment were called down upon his life. The point is that a woman's power, or any massive power that has no discipline or control, can do much harm. Girls, you already possess power that enables you to accomplish your tasks and goals, and fulfill all your needs. Discovering and refining this power takes time. The power you possess can do good and attract good, or do harm and attract trouble and woe. Learn how to use your existing beauty, intellect, talents, skills, abilities and beliefs in virtuous ways, which will attract what you are looking for. Your entire impression should be inviting, and not be used in an aggressive, controlling or manipulative manner. Don't be an Amazon here. I have seen pretty women use their beauty in arrogant or controlling ways, which diminished what seemed beautiful at first glance, then turned out to be very ugly indeed. Their careless outward actions, stemming from inward neglect, minimized their beauty. True femininity, when it is real and natural, is beautiful to look upon. To add to it by exaggeration, over-embellishment or overacting, is not necessary, and actually detracts from it. I have also seen women who, instead of just being themselves, act out being overly sexy and alluring, using methods such as improper dressing, speaking or exaggerated walking. Many young ladies unknowingly detract from themselves through fowl language, masculine dressing, and male-like thinking. By contrast, I have seen women who were extremely beautiful, comfortable with themselves, not adding to it overtly, but being open, gentle, warm and loving to all those around, and they are the rulers of all they survey. This adds to a woman's attraction significantly, and is pleasant, not only for men, but for admiring women as well. When the inner and outer beauties match up, everyone takes note.

Learn who you are, what your gifts and talents can do, then master them as great ballet dancers and ice skaters do. The world you want to live in will be yours for the taking, if you find favor with God and man. Favor is found by correctly appreciating and using the gifts you were given. The feminine strength is right there under your nose, and is your greatest built-in strength. It is already programmed to seek out the masculine in the opposite sex, so go with its naturally intended flow. Discover it, let it come out and about, play with it and let it help you become the girl or woman you were meant to be, and have fun doing it. There is nothing wrong with visiting and playing with your masculine side, but I don't recommend it for attracting the opposite sex. By this I mean, there will be physical tasks that may bring out your masculine side, times to practice self-preservation, and times to just let your hair down. Be aware that if you act or dress in a masculine way, you will attract the dynamics that accompany what you are practicing. For instance, playing up your masculine side could attract the more feminine results found in weak men. Unless you are looking for a feminine male or a weak man for a life companion, this is not something you want to do. You will always be playing a role in conflict with your true self. For those of you who are looking for a true man and are open to becoming a true woman in the process, use what you have in the way of your softness and femininity, because no true man wants a masculine girl or a weak woman. When you learn to use what's in your true nature, you will be overwhelmed with right results, and when you find the inward life of your own hidden kingdom, you will be more beautiful than ever you thought possible.

Girl Pearl: *Peace comes from within. Do not seek it without.*

Woman's Intuition is Not Superstition

Let me start off by saying that a woman's intuition is not an urban myth or a legend. It is real and is a gift to women from their great ancestor Eve, who got it from the Creator. It is earthy, meaning it's down-to-earth and fundamental, doing what it's supposed to do. It's an exceptional navigational tool. It's your informant, adviser, communicator, expert witness and revealing mechanism, all in one. Women have proved to be very sensitive to it, and often regret ignoring it or not allowing it to speak. In the wholesome roles women play on this planet, it's no accident they've been given this ability in an extra dose or two. It could be considered one of the greatest inward gifts of all, and could it be bottled, would outsell coca-cola, milk, water, and alcoholic beverages. It is coveted and effective, and ladies…it is yours for free.

In order to take advantage of this marvelous gift, you must first listen to it, then act on, and obey it. As situations present themselves, let your intuition introduce them to you. Learn to trust what you see and know, and inquire further along those lines. It wants to work and serve you if you let it. Remain aware, open, and observing, and you'll receive input from everything around you. As a caution, when you ignore or override your intuition, it will become dull, and eventually you may lose touch with it entirely, leading you into the world of confusion and doubt. Upon entering that realm, you begin to doubt yourself even more. Guard this inward gift by engaging and using it. This is how you show respect for it and, of course, honor to the one who supplied it. In time and with practice, your intuition will preserve, protect, and reward you nonstop for the rest of your life.

Make friends and learn to co-exist with this unique gift. Be advised that the natural enemies of intuition are doubt, confusion, and analysis. It helps to know that the very first impression that presents itself to you in a situation is usually the most accurate. The nonsense follows after that. Ladies, start your engines every day with this by trusting in what you see and know. If you can appreciate this paragraph, your intuition is doing just fine.

Girl Pearl: How wonderful to know the things a woman knows...sharing with men is optional.

Wherever You Go, Take Your Heart Too

There are some people in college who don't want to be there; others can't stand their place of employment; still others tend children reluctantly (their own, or others) and simply go through the motions and put up with all of it. A guy at a department store answers the phone, and you know by his voice he hates his job. What about less than favorable interactions with family members? Do you go along with what you know to be wrong just to keep the peace? Do you say and do things that are not real or sincere for various reasons you consider appropriate? You keep the gossip and confusion going if you do. You know it, they know it, and what is the point in doing so? What do you get out of helping, visiting or interacting with family when you don't like doing it? We see this happening all over the place. If you are doing this, stop it! If your heart is not in what you are doing, everyone suffers for it, including you. Stop making excuses for dishonest behaviors. It is dysfunctional and leads to more of the same.

Typical dysfunctional answers for some of these examples are: *but I need the money and the benefits are good*; *I can't find anything else; this is all I know, I don't want to hurt anyone's feelings; I just didn't want to stir things up; this is not my problem,* and on and on. So what does one do if they are in a dysfunctional situation, bad relationship or friendship? Telling yourself that you are only going to do this for a short while and that it's only temporary, makes you out to be the phony one. In other words, you are putting up with it because you have a hidden reason for doing so. Perhaps you think it will pass with time? How about you are expecting it to correct itself? There are so many ways to avoid the reality. So you say to yourself that you have to work to pay the bills, and your job is not what you love most. Well, it shouldn't be what you love most, but as long as it is what you are doing, until something better comes along, put your whole heart in it....be the best at it, make your day count for good, for however long you must be there. If not, then you're not real. In fact, you are part of the problem. Here is what I am getting at. If you go somewhere, go with all your heart, and give all you've got to give. If you do something, do it with all your heart. If your heart is missing, so are you. If you have something to say that you think is worthy and will make a difference, speak it with all your heart. If not, what are you doing here? Going along to get along is not real, and is no good for you or the people around you. Do something about how you interact and perceive your environment, and your surroundings will change. Sourpuss in, sourpuss out. Contribution and caring in, contribution and caring comes out. You choose, and whatever it is you choose, bet the heart. It's a sure win. People who do this tend to leave an impression that stays with others all their lifetimes. If you were operating at one hundred percent wherever you went, just imagine the results that would follow.

Girl Pearl: We may sometimes not know what love is, but at all times we know what it isn't.

Each Day Counts, But Don't Count Days

Everyday is a good day. Who is telling you otherwise? What makes you think there is more to the day than the day itself? Look how it starts: You wake up in the morning and a day is awaiting you. What a fantastic premise...what a gift to give someone. A day! Who, but God, can give such gifts? *Here's a day for you to spend any way you want.* I suspect the meaning of receiving the day has been lost. Perhaps we skip the

99

appreciation part, the very part that gives it meaning and purpose. You see, you have been invited to participate in another day, and it's a day you have never experienced before. This is not to be mocked, wasted, criticized or misused by grumbling, complaining, or being in a *bad mood.* Unfortunately, we do just that. How about a *thank you for inviting me to today* moment? Days are not meant to be perfect or problem free. They are meant to teach or show us something; they are to be lived and experienced. Not since the beginning of creation have any two days, or any two people been the same, nor will they ever be....wow, oh wow. Each is unique in its construction. Let this trickle down from your brain onto your tongue and into your soul. No two days are alike. That means value.

How do you start your day? The birds all over this planet start their day with a song that says many things. *I am here! I am happy to see the morning light! I am in love! I am looking for something!...I AM.* Then, the rest of nature follows suit. Plants open up slowly to receive the new day and partake of it by blossoming wide. They drink deeply and heartily from the sun, wind and rain. Trees are fixed in their places, yet move constantly as the wind rustles, detangles and thins out their leaves, allowing new growth to appear, and rejoicing in the elements that were given. Consider that something magnificent is at work here. The systems that we take for granted on this planet may escape some, but let us begin to acknowledge them with awe and respect. The natural recycling of water is another of these wondrous systems. Consider that the same water is being used over and over again since creation of this planet, through a system of recycling that boggles the mind. Dinosaurs drank the same water. Yet, you can always count on it, and we do. Other elements do their parts as well. The wind kicks up and participates in the day's work of moving and tossing things around. It is like an invisible servant on a secret mission. No one knows where it came from, what it is doing, or where it is going, but it is on the ball unceasingly. There's a lot going on and you have been invited to participate. Here is a day for you to spend. Spend it wisely.

The hustle bustle of everyday life is upon us now more than ever. When we awaken, our minds race to meet up with our thoughts, and mentally go through the day's list of where we must go and what must be done, then we prepare for the journey. We jump in the shower, do all our necessaries, dress for success, coffee up and hit the road. The day I am describing is a typical day. Is there anything that makes it special or stand out from yesterday or last week? We find ourselves rushing from destination to arrival, only to leave again. But did you take in the journey? Did you notice the detail in the simple things? Did you set aside moments to reflect or look around wherever you went? Did you notice others coming to and fro just like you? Did you hear or see anything special to make this day different? It is different than any other day because, like you, it has never been here before. How about you? Did you contribute to something or someone so at the end of this day, someone else was touched by you? Did you give whatever you had? Perhaps a smile, a kind word, or holding the door for someone?

I often come across well dressed people who pride themselves on looking and giving their best. You've seen them too. I take the time to acknowledge them because they took the time to present themselves. This exchange is time well spent for both. You can go through your days in a way that they all look alike, or you can mark each day with a special memory. You have many chances in a day to create something by your words and actions that gives something of yourself back to the day that was given to you. Be available, seeking and aware. You meet people all day, and if you don't seize every moment, your potential date may come and go, or perhaps your true love passed you by, but you were too busy or preoccupied to meet him. Opportunities abound, and you must be ready to seize them!

Instead of rushing from point A to point B, next time you get up in the morning, can you please just take a moment to realize, very simply, that you've been given a day, the gift of gifts, to spend however you like? Whoever gives days for gifts should be thanked and given honor and glory, for this Giver is worthy to receive it. When this is expressed through gratitude,

101

acknowledgment, and by using the gift, the gift Giver is automatically thanked, honored, and included in the process.

Girl Pearl: Treasure each other in the recognition that we don't know how long we shall have each other.

The School of Life

I'm going to submit to you something for your consideration that's worthy of a second look. So often, with all our growing adult responsibilities, we get caught up in being too serious, responsible, willful, and focused on the obvious, that is, the pursuit of food, shelter and clothing. What happens is that joy, fun, mystery and adventure have been weeded out of our lives. The moment we are in becomes affected (or infected) and carried into the next moment and the next, until even the big picture is affected by what has become a monotonous routine, where we're not living, but merely existing.

We must keep a healthy balance in all we do in order to thrive and journey through life. Next time you wake up in the morning, remind yourself that school has begun. The school of life. At the end of your day, before you go to bed, school of life lets out. You can easily get too serious about life out of ignorance, busyness, unawareness and lack of knowledge. Rather than educating ourselves by seeking and asking questions, some of us choose to remain unchanged and dormant, and before you're aware of it, worry sets in and emotions begin taking charge of your decisions. This results in mood swings and roller-coaster ups and downs. It may feel great when you're on a high, but every new high creates a new low, and what goes up must come down. Aim for a more predictable and steady flow. In going about your daily work, let the adult in you supervise the inner child, but let the inner child do the work, because kids know how to have fun. The results will be that everything gets done, fun is sighted and supported, and you have more energy, because it was not spent on your emotions. People are lifted up, motivated, and encouraged when the child in them comes out. There is no reason to hang out in a serious, stress-filled, willful state of mind. Don't take on more than you can handle. Only take on what is for you, and take your time with it when you do. The kid in you not only knows what to do, but has a ball doing it. Support that, and the adult in you will also be very happy. Seek recess, not excess.

Girl Pearl: *To have that happy grownup female feeling...is called being a woman. When you add a confident smile to it, the world is yours...*

Rule Playing or Rule Slaying?

You obey the speed limit (I hope). However, there are people who do not. They will pass you up and an interesting thing happens. One of you is wrong and one of you is right. Playing by the rules give us a predictable outcome. Not playing by the rules causes the dynamics to change. Then, everyone involved has to take a look at what they are doing and why. Let's remember that the nature of every activity, organization and game, is defined by rules.

Throughout this book, the Judeo-Christian ethics, rules, beliefs and perspectives have been applied. Adhering to, and obeying them works. Not only will you get good results in doing so, but will find favor with yourself, with others and with God. Self-assessment is wise, and denying or ignoring what you see in this assessment, is not. When playing checkers, chess, and monopoly, if we stray from the known and acceptable way, we are no longer playing the games that we understood and agreed to play. These principles also apply to sports activities.

Different sports have different rules, and to play outside them, calls down fouls or penalties.

Workplace rules are designed to protect the employees, insurance requirements, and business plans. Failure to agree and practice them brings unnecessary risk to everyone, and those who go against them are labeled rogues, or rebels. This may seem *cool* to you, but it is not a productive way to gain respect or attention. There's not much room for misapplication of traffic laws, or the results would be (and are) disastrous. Chaos and accidents ensue when the rules of the road are ignored or broken. Even in the realm of fine dining there are rules designed to enhance the experience. I learned to perfect them by watching others in order to fully enjoy it.

Rule players: please be advised that by adhering to and practicing the rules of whatever you are doing, you have set an example, and your very act or deed makes the non-rule player stand out like a sore thumb. Correction of that person is being demonstrated by your actions.

Non-rule players: as long as you practice your own set of rules amongst those that are in conformity, you will be continually swimming against the tide. Big energy drain too! When you are outed for your behavior, you will have to face the consequences of it. What kind of life are you making for yourself when you must keep explaining, defending and arguing as to why you are not in obedience? If you won't or can't play by the rules, your rebellion is being acted out. This is living life backwards. You are out of the flow, and creating problems for yourself and others.

When we come together as cities, counties and states, and have large masses of people, the needs of the many will always outweigh and dominate the needs of the few. When you are in the comfort of your own home or property, then you may stretch those private legs of yours all you want. **Rules defined**: *prescribed guide for conduct or action; something that governs behavior.* Are you a rule player, or a rule slayer? A theme that stands out in the Bible, is the breaking or keeping of God's laws. On one side there is great reward, and on the other is a great price to pay. Many times situations arise requiring activation and deployment of common sense, which may conflict with known and/or outdated rules and regulations, and these are exceptions. Also, as rules are to help us and give us guidance in society and among our fellow men, let us never forget that each of us carries within us a mechanism in the form of a moral compass that guides our behavior. Each of us has constant access to it, and none of us can deny when it stirs. As you learn to recognize and obey your inner prompts, the outer part, as well as everything else, follows naturally.

Girl Pearl: *The happiness of love is in action.*

'How' and 'Why' Must Never Die

Do you remember as a child when you reached the young and inquisitive age where you started asking a lot of questions? Why do they put headstones on graves? Why is everything so green? How does the ocean know to stop at the shore? How does a baby get in mommy's stomach? Parents and teachers joke about having to deal with this, but perhaps it is not a laughing matter. Well, if the questions were easy and the timing was right, you got them answered most of the time. If not, you were either ignored or given an answer to make you quiet, rather than feed your inquiry. If your questions continue to go unanswered or ignored, over time the *how* and the *why* begin to weaken, as you are programmed to not ask anymore. **THINK**: What happens to a muscle that is not used? Atrophy or shrinkage begins. The result of not answering our children is similar. We *dumb down* our children and ourselves by not exploring the mysteries and wonders that surround us wherever we go, when all we have to do is simply use the *how* and the *why*. In addition, we do not use all our talents and skills, and of course, only limited parts of the brain. Perhaps we did not follow our inner instructions? Impatient adults often respond to a child's question of *"why?"* with the answer: *"because."* This is not an answer, nor was it ever an answer. It is merely a polite way of saying…*shut up* and *not now*. If you have ever stayed indoors for hours, or were in a dark room and then emerged, all of your senses came alive as though someone had turned on a switch. This is what happens when you use and feed the *how* and the *why* mechanisms in yourself and others. In return, they reward you for using them with peace and satisfaction, and by dispensing even more curiosity to you. The Giver and Supporter of this is also pleased for having invested and participated in the building and feeding of your inquiry. All that is required of you, is to use what you already have, then more will be given. Your *how* and *why* were given to introduce you to, and help you develop your identity, skills, and talents, which will eventually lead to your calling in life and a very satisfying journey. All the promises of God come-a-calling eagerly to his children who ask *how* and *why*. He wants you to know, and he wants to be the one to tell you. He stands waiting for your inquisitiveness to

106

Girl Pearl: *Reaching out and exploring makes innocence more adoring…*

awaken so he can first give you the question, then reward you with the answer!

As we mature, most of us begin searching more diligently for meaning and purpose. We begin to realize we are missing something, but can't quite put our finger on what it is we're missing. Perhaps we are looking for the *"Yes!"* or *"Ah ha!"* experience? Asking questions is the beginning of a worthy pursuit of this, but sadly, has become somewhat of a lost art and often discouraged practice. We came into the world with this wonderful gift, then succumbed to not using it. Turn this up and put it to good use. This allows you to fine tune and focus your journey to receive the optimum from every experience. Begin asking questions of others concerning things that are of interest to you. Be prepared for people's impatience and programming, and the world's attempts to discourage you. Become even more intrigued as to *why* they are acting defensively or impatiently, and *how* to go about responding to those reactions. Practice patience in return, and stay on mission until you have your answers, seeking as many sources as are necessary to get them. As you begin to learn about others, you will discover the little jewels and the not so bright things at work inside of you. Then, you can enhance the glitter, or that which is good, and eliminate the dull, or that which is not so good. Even more importantly, you'll discover your true identity which comes with time and practice. You will find as you continue with this, that others will begin to approach you with questions. Now it is your chance to pay into the system and help someone else. Of course, you get fed too. The system is brilliant if you use it. Someone went to great trouble and detail to set this all up and *install* it in you, and someone else went to great detail and trouble to make sure that no one could steal it from you. The Creator of the *how and why* system will perform, but only if you practice and listen to your common sense, your moral compass, and the inquisitive little kid in you who wants to know things and wants to seek and share about them. You must do your part to receive it. Ask, seek, knock and it will be given to you.

Pssst!...Your Blindside is Showing

Who, me? Yes, you!

There are things we do consciously and purposely throughout the day, both in personal and business venues, which trigger cause and effect. Hopefully, we are doing the right things, and if you monitor yourself, you will know. But what if you did not know and proceeded to think all was well. Let's look at this for a moment. Results don't lie, and they tell the story, whatever that story is. They are the proof that your beliefs are working. It's that simple. RESULTS DON'T LIE. Lack of results don't lie either, but here lies the problem: Something invisible is at work which is interfering with our normal life's agenda, but what is it? It's *denial*. Denial is a strong weapon your ego employs with the help of your pride to keep you unaware. If you give in to it, it begins to dull you, and before you know it, you have a blindside. This is an area you cannot see, but others see without any problem. Because you trust yourself and like to figure things out, you are not quick to admit that anything is wrong with you, but to the contrary, you think the problem lies with everyone other than you. This is the blindside working its dark magic on you, which you buy into without question.

When you take time to remain open, when you desire to know the truth even if it hurts your pride, then and only then, do you come against this blindness and stand a chance to see properly. We must keep in mind that we need feedback and input from others in order to monitor ourselves for the parts we cannot see. Seeing your blindside allows you to have *rest* from all that is wrong with you. I am choosy whom I ask for feedback, help or input, but am not at all above asking when I need it. Exercise caution as to whom you become vulnerable when you begin to investigate, but definitely open up and ask. Your skills, talents and intelligence can only take you so far, and it is wise to seek counsel among those whose lives you respect. Interacting correctly with our like-kind benefits all of us, and hones us into a razor-sharp existence. It could be referred to as *evolving*, and the system works if you use it.

Be prepared to receive truth, recognizing that while it may be painful or unpleasant, it is well worth attaining, and will compliment your journey in life. After acquiring your cherished and wanted feedback and input, if you find yourself arguing over it, you have defeated both the purpose and the process. Again, your pride and ego at work, and with your permission and cooperation, robbing you of growth. Let the truth go to work. If it is painful, realize it is short-term and will be rewarding in the long-term. Do not argue when comments are made that you have asked for. Merely receive them, thank the commenter, then move on. If it is for you, your insides will confirm it. If it is not for you, it rolls away like water off a duck's back.

Also, it is interesting to consider that people from whom you ask feedback will sometimes, without knowing it, comment on themselves while they are answering you. Thus, they are giving *themselves* feedback and input by interacting with you. They may know it then, or perhaps realize it later, but the point is, they may be speaking for themselves also. Whether it is for themselves or you, let it come out for both your sakes. That's the key. Stop paying no mind to being blind. You are greater than that, so go toward the constructive criticism of those who can see what you cannot. God was well-pleased when he made you and me. Let's do our part.

Girl Pearl: Be clear on this point: Being a woman is a very powerful thing to be. You must learn to use this power wisely and for the right reasons.

Loneliness is Very Painful

A very real subject of concern to many, is loneliness. The state and condition of being alone. That everyone wants to be loved, and no one wants to be alone, is the human condition. Since the creation of the first man, this has never changed. To some, the pain of being lonely is nearly unbearable. Women have needs that must be addressed in the mental, emotional, psychological, spiritual, and physical realms. These needs are very real, and must never be ignored. In fact, denial and neglect bring on painful experiences of their own, as they tend to amplify the present conditions. Ladies, we must not cope with the realm of loneliness in a needy way, but in a way that compliments you and your journey. This is not a complex subject unless we make it so. When you were a child, remember how easy it was to interact with others, and to play and have fun? Loneliness wasn't even a consideration. Less thinking and more doing were the dynamics. Those same dynamics will work today also. Playing in kindergarten took no planning. Someone threw you the ball and you threw it back. Now, you discover as young girls or adults, there are other dynamics at play, which go deeper and become very meaningful. To want to share your personality, your thoughts, feelings and contributions with others, and theirs with you, is one of the great, satisfying joys of life. Intimacy, the personal act of two people getting to know each other, comes in stages, with each stage requiring mutual participation. To truly know someone is a very worthy, purposeful, and meaningful endeavor. No two people are alike, which makes for a fascinating experience with everyone you meet. The way we go about it, is what I want you to look at. Loneliness doesn't have to exist. It is something to confront with inquisitiveness and interest, which will result in fun, exploration, adventure and meaning. If you go about it because of neediness, you will not gain what the process was meant to teach you, nor will you be attractive to those around you. Use this difficult time wisely, to find contentedness and peace, and learn about yourself. Every woman has beautiful secrets hidden deep within her that become even more beautiful as they unfurl in a mysterious and wonderful way to her prince charming. Until she is able to blossom in this way, she feels lonely, because she and her secrets are the only two involved.

Occupying your time with self-improvement, career, schooling, volunteering or chores, will alleviate some of the pain and also contribute to a sense of daily well-being. I should mention one of my personal favorites is to share with a good friend. How much and how far, depends on what kind of friendship you have. A true friend is usually someone who likes you a lot, even to the point of loving you. In that realm of love and friendship, much can be done as we encourage one another from day to day. There is nothing like a good share and care session with a friend. These suggestions will never address the secret place in your heart where you want to share with another, and to love and be loved, but they will allow you to make forward and meaningful progress on the subject matter. Keep something in mind. You are not looking for just any old remedy to your existence. You want a purposeful life, with meaning and depth. For that reason, you want your standards of sharing to have a high degree of trust and vulnerability. You must never give that away easily, and never until you have found a person who is credible and worthy of your trust. If you have done so in the past, then you can identify with why you shouldn't. I am sure we can both agree that it stings and produces hurt. So it is better to store up the quality feelings and ideas, then patiently await the opportunity to share with someone who can and will appreciate them in confidence.

Although you may experience bouts of deep loneliness as you seek, pursue, and address your true calling, you are never alone while doing so. As long as you live, you are able to do something about whatever comes up in your life, so look for every opportunity to do so, and use that adventure as a good reason to get up every morning with purpose in your heart. When those waves of loneliness overtake you, allow them to come without adding or taking away from them, and let your heart be poured out when they do. This is a call to God. Go toward the suffering and realize you are suffering for the right reasons. After all, you haven't filled up the void with meaningless relationships, and didn't sell out to something less than love. In patience, you are waiting for the real love to arrive. So during this time of loneliness, remember that you are being prepared and changed from the inside out, as is the one intended

113

for you. Use this time to your advantage, being grateful for having time alone that allows this cleansing to take place in you. It is necessary. If we are to be given the desires of our hearts in God's way (and not our way), then in patience we must first learn to find contentment in whatever state we find ourselves.

Apply the principle of *short-term pain, long-term pleasure* to the subject of loneliness. To make the point, consider that many women go through a relatively short period of hell to bring a baby into this world, for long-term pleasure. It is a befitting example of the principle in action. As you suffer loneliness while looking for the right man, in time you will have the long-term reward, and since patience acquires itself in patience, you will have mastered that realm as well. In time, all things will come about as they were meant to. Oh, what joy when you do find that one-and-only-someone, and what a delightful surprise awaits him to receive the mystery of *you!* Keep the deep and intimate secrets for that day, and when it arrives, because you have suffered long and endured loneliness patiently and in a purposeful way, how much more grateful and appreciative you will be to receive the one you waited so long to love. Until he arrives, remember there is consolation for all, and in fact, the *same* consolation for all.

Girl Pearl: *All men who avoid female society have dull perceptions and are stupid, or have gross tastes and revolt against what is pure.* - Thackeray

The Two Greatest Pains

When the pain of loneliness is greater than the pain of rejection, one will seek the lesser pain, which is rejection. If the pain of being rejected is greater than being lonely, one will seek loneliness as the lesser pain. Thank God for this dynamic,

114

because it can help you summon the strength to bust out of yourself, similar to a seed coming out of its shell, and not unlike a baby chick pecking away to crack the egg it's in. You cannot gain unless you risk. I want you to learn to go toward your pain, sorrow, and fears, because right on the other side of all that lies your freedom and reward.

As you test and go through this process, you are going to make mistakes, and you may even be judged for them. You may suffer from someone's cruelty (intended or not) and this is part of the process of maturing and developing a second skin. Imagine a sunburn to sensitive skin. Once it has become tan, it is no longer a painful experience. So it is with the pain of your mistakes, the cruelty of others, and the fear of taking risks.

I have encountered those so afraid of life that they have chosen to go through it alone, allowing themselves to be robbed of companionship. There are times it is a conscious, personal choice, made for the right reasons. If, however, the decision is wrought out of fear of rejection or lack of confidence, it is unhealthy and very apparent in those who suffer from it. They don't look or sound well, their body language is not inviting, and they may stare at the ground or far off into space. Their hygiene may be in question, along with an unkempt presentation of themselves. What they are saying is "leave me alone because I do not know what to do." The very message they are putting out indicates a need for something. This is their distorted way of calling out that they want to love and be loved, and do not want to be alone. They know this too, but cannot express it as such, so out of fear of rejection, they sabotage any chance of love by pre-empting its possibility. It is not uncommon to find people being influenced by dark forces and powers that rule by convenience, neediness and opportunity. Convenience, because these forces are in the right place at the right time to take advantage; neediness, because it causes you to want something before your time or out of your flow, allowing wrong answers and remedies to tempt you with questionable solutions; and opportunity is established for these forces to have a go at you when you've given up or are unavailable to God, and the right way is not being pursued. These forces keep you ignorant, distracted and comfortably, miserably *safe*.

Keep in mind we were not put here to be defeated. You are not a plant, insect or animal, all of which act mostly out of instinct and environmental response. You have a greater responsibility for your actions. You've been made with a consciousness that demands you seek, knock, ask, investigate, and yearn for whatever it is you are looking for. Obstacles and pain only test how badly you want these things, and whether you will continue in the pursuit of your desires. They are not designed to stop you. Only you can stop you. God's promises cannot be thwarted or interfered with, except by not accepting them. In today's world however, navigating through the different circumstances can be challenging, and may cause one to give in and give up if not approached correctly.

Girl Pearl: Hate is love looking for itself everyplace except where love is.

Doubt and Confusion are an Intrusion

Who among us has not encountered, suffered from, or practiced being in doubt and confusion? These are the enemies of mankind, out to rob you of all that is yours, yet they attain victory over you because you let them. Their source of power comes from lack of awareness on your part, by having little or no faith, and by an innocent ignorance. Other than that, they have no power of their own. It was never intended for you to be robbed, deprived or tricked as you journey.

Remember, it all started out pleasant enough. God wished Adam a happy birthday and the planet earth was given to him to subdue. That is our heritage. *Enjoy the planet earth and do great things* was our mandate. Think about it. Mankind is the most superior being on this planet, having consciousness and awareness far superior to all other life forms. Furthermore, we are suited to be stewards (receivers) of this great planet, having the ability to nurture, protect, expand, develop, and motivate all that we see, hear, and have. So, how can there be any doubt and confusion built into this life system? There cannot be. It is an outside distraction, brought about by dark forces intent on robbing, deceiving, and destroying your good works and purpose. They were not part of creation, but entered in under dishonorable circumstances. Although these forces cannot stop you, they can put up roadblocks and detours as you travel. Not to worry, your built-in guidance systems, where God communes with mankind, function just fine and cannot be tampered with. Listening to that small, still, gentle voice within you, works. Being still and calm will allow you to hear it. Learning to discipline your mind and emotions is time well spent. The first step to freedom and to reclaiming your rights is to realize these truths and begin to practice them. As you become aware of yourself and draw closer to the truth about yourself, then what you do and why you do it become self-evident. Then, rewards from doing your part follow shortly thereafter. These negative systems can help you grow stronger when you do not react to them, but just watch and observe them instead. Their agenda is thwarted by being observed, especially by innocence.

Do not doubt what you know to be right in your heart. If you saw someone periodically approaching a flower bed and taking flowers that did not belong to them, and you said nothing, this behavior would continue until there were no flowers left. If, however, you said "hey, what are you doing there…leave those flowers alone," then it would stop right there and then. You have spoken up for the right reason, the flowers are protected, and the one doing the destruction (thieving) is outed and thwarted. Be the person who speaks up for the right wherever you go, and in everything you do. Replace doubt and confusion with faith. By discontinuing the use of one, the other is activated. If not you, who? If not now, when? Continue on this path and you will discover many rewards and hidden secrets which are given and revealed only to those who

117

demonstrate they can handle responsibility. Pretty soon, you will come to realize that it's easier to speak up than not to. Remember, if you have something to say, say it. Short, sweet and to the point. Remember to include compassion (charity) which is *how* you say it, and anything is allowed. If you have something to do, do it. Hesitation and over-analyzing only support and invite back your old nemesis, doubt and confusion, where everything goes on hold, then quickly downhill. Practice righting wrongs. You will make mistakes, but you will learn and grow because your motives are pure and decent, and the Universe will honor this. Have faith in this system. It has been working and was here before you got here. Join it and you will find satisfaction in all you do, even unto the small and minor things. Do not be fooled, and be of good cheer as you investigate your God-given rights. The end result will be that doubt and confusion will weaken, be put in their places, and eventually diminish and vanish. Faith will be active and working in you while you are seeking opportunities to practice and grow. You will not journey alone, for the one who created the system is pleased and will join you when you follow his instructions. He is waiting for you now.

Girl Pearl: Love is a very confusing part of life that makes a lot of sense.

Knowledge Casts Out Fear

Knowledge on any subject begins to replace fear of that subject, specifically the fear of the unknown. Once you begin an inquiry into a subject you don't understand, and begin to experience and learn about it, your fears of it are dispelled, and in some cases, you become empowered. Do this with any subject you are resisting or hesitating going toward. Ask questions, learn something about it, and you have bettered yourself in that field. Do this with many things, and when you start becoming informed, then *own* what you have learned, that

118

is to say, don't doubt it. Do this in humility, coupled with confidence, and do it with all your heart. As you gain experience through life and in your chosen field, you will exceed "owning" the behavior, and will then qualify to enter into mastery of it. This is a very attractive thing to see at work in someone. Ignorance is a choice, and it can be replaced by a better choice. I am not referring to a high intelligence or genius, just a simple awareness and application to everything and anything you do. Perform like you are special, and you will be treated special in return. The opposite applies too. Everyone is ignorant coming into the world. Mankind is currently set up so that a journey is required to unravel mystery and purpose. You must learn, and as you do, your worth and confidence levels grow accordingly. Do this like a child, full of wonder and awe, open to whatever will happen next. Look forward to every instance, and the faith you develop from living this life casts out fear automatically. Fear was never meant to be part of your real journey. It is a learned behavior, and exists so you can discover that it is not to your liking, and choose otherwise. If you must fear something, until you can replace it with the proper life ingredients, fear not living life, being ignorant, and letting your gifts and talents go unused. None of that for you.

Fear of success, failure, intimacy and rejection, support and bring about low self-esteem. These are all are standing in line to have their shot at you if you let them. They want to stop you, rob you, sabotage you, and keep you from having the desires of your heart and the promises of God. What makes them so problematic is they are not easy to identify, nor are they readily seen. Others see these fears in you and you may glimpse them as you travel. If you give in to these imposters, they will gladly oblige you. Do not do so. Here is where you may need to do a little work. Once you discover these fears, either through feedback, input or self-realization, then you must take steps to come to the origins of them, which begins the process to eliminate or correct them. The origin of my own fears came from feelings of unworthiness to have, to be good enough to have, or to be secure in having, anything good. Low self-esteem was the result of compound childhood episodes which had been hidden away within me for years. Most problems we face in our lives arise from childhood trauma. Our parents were first up to guide and nurture us, and they had never raised children before. So, you either got all they had, or the best of what they had, whatever that was. Trauma which has not been corrected is handed down to future generations. Either way, damage crept into all of us, person to person and generation to generation, making us realize how far...yes, how far we have fallen. Yet, thanks be to God, there is a way to correct and direct it...he gave us a way back.

Going toward your fears causes them to come into the light for self-examination and, more importantly, to be judged by the light of truth. No darkness, nor foul deed can stand to be in this cleansing, purifying light for too long without fleeing or being sentenced. That's where you need to go to expose and confront *who you are* once and for all. Hiding, evading or pretending will lead to denial, which is even more painful and high maintenance than the process of ridding yourself of fear. So, go toward your fears, and suffer while doing so, realizing you've already suffered the woe (deserved or not) of remaining in them. While you repent and seek change in the moment, the nonsense and dysfunction must flee. Before it was you who ran away by denial, evasions or disguises...now you are reversing the system. This time, you stay and it goes, rather than you go and it stays. This process may take time, but it is well worth it. You must seek out and go toward, no *run* toward, any truth about yourself, no matter how horrifying, which might reveal to you your true condition.

Dating or marrying before this condition is resolved, will not attract your true potentials, but will attract others with dysfunctions fitting to yours. Like answers unto like. The blind and the hurting attract the blind and the hurting. You don't want to be attracted to others for their dysfunction. Everyone has fears to some degree, but be of good cheer...you were not born with these fears and you don't have to continue with them. Either you acquired them or they bullied their way into your life. Once you handle and disarm them, you'll be free to experience life the way it was meant to be. The negative programming we all picked up along the way has to go bye-bye.

In its place, your innocence and common sense will be allowed to return to guide you as intended.

Girl Pearl: Too many of us stay walled up because we are afraid of getting hurt. We are afraid to care too much for fear that the other person doesn't care at all.

Stop Taking Excuse Making 101

Pride can work against you. If you argue, make excuses, blame, explain or defend excessively, pride is upon you. In this mode, you will learn nothing and know everything...all wrong. You will not advance and you will even be robbed of a true experience. Watch this in yourself. If you find yourself arguing during the conversation process, you will get to keep your argument, and of course nothing ventured nothing gained. In other words, what you might have received was not able to enter, because there was something else in its place, occupying the space. You must risk what is in there now, and if it holds, you will keep it. If it fails, boot it out and replace it with something that works. Remain open, risk vulnerability and consider that pride is at work. To counter this within ourselves, asking questions about any subject matter you are experiencing, shifts the dynamics in our favor. Keep asking until you are satisfied with an answer and the outcome. You see, during the time you are asking questions, you have come out of your mind, and have begun probing into the moment at hand. You are now a seeker, and people who seek find things. Keep seeking until you find specifically what you are looking for. The very process I'm describing, when implemented correctly, is an enemy of pride. Remember, that which is *not* good for you lives in the shadows, and that which *is* good for you is transparent and out in the light. Help bring everything into the light, and the only thing that will get hurt is your pride and your wrongdoing. From there, things get better, lighter, and easier to receive and

121

understand. You do not need pride or its systems when you have understanding and knowing. Accept the truth, feel its sting of correction, be glad for it and move on. Repeat this all the days of your life, until you have reached the point where God in you is guiding your every move.

Girl Pearl: *Love is to be spent, not saved.*

Yelling, Screaming, Smoking & Cursing?

No.....not allowed if you are reaching for optimum. Have your private moments and occasions where if this has to take place, there are little or no repercussions from it. Go into your closet and have at it if you must. I have heard things yelled by women during intense labor of childbirth that sailors would be embarrassed to hear. This was the only place I thought it was excusable. It doesn't look good, sound good, or bring out the good in anyone, man, woman or child, to be cursing, yelling, or screaming. Your personal stock as a woman goes down significantly. Sorry, but this has got to be tamed, especially in public. Also, a woman smoking is not very attractive, and as a man, I wouldn't want to compete with a cigarette. I want to know the woman, not the smoke. Ladies, this is not too much to ask, and if you are doing any of these things, stop it now. If you have not done these things, then don't start! Remember, we are publicly relating ourselves, and this conduct, cursing, smoking and screaming, asks too much from the people who have to deal with it. In the end, if you don't learn to correct this, you will lose credibility and respect by practicing it.

A true man would not conduct himself by yelling, screaming, smoking and cursing in your presence. If a male is not ashamed to do so, it's time to look at yourself. In many cases, a woman either commands respect or allows disrespect. Men gauge their audience before allowing this to come through.

If someone is ashamed to practice bad behavior in your presence, you are doing something right.

Now, as to piercing your body, applying tattoos, dying your hair multiple colors and wearing gladiator outfits, you're sending a particular message, and it is being conveyed. What is your message? Are you aware of what you are saying by these actions? It is a fair question. I am not condemning you, but wondering how it benefits you. Many, who have not yet discovered their true identities, have succumbed to the "quick solution" to the identity question, by creating false identities in various forms and substituting them in place of realness. The *self* is a prize that does not need to be added to or taken away from, and there is a correct way to compliment it. Adding things to your body to get noticed, takes away from who you really are, and begins to develop and enhance a false self. When you accept and love yourself, you love the One who sent you here, and he, in turn, causes you to flourish. We are off to a good start when that happens.

Girl Pearl: *There is no worse evil than a bad woman; and nothing has ever been produced better than a good one.*
- *Euripides*

Being Guilt Driven is Not Livin'

Being guilt driven is purely the by-product of bad choices and wrong decisions. Compound guilt comes from repeating behavior you know is wrong. Attempting to alleviate the process incorrectly creates another guilt. To clarify my point, imagine that something is nagging and bothering you, and you're able to trace it to your recent past behavior. Instead of bearing the responsibility for this behavior and letting it lead you to repentance, you continue with more of the same behavior that brought about the guilt in the first place. By doing so, you continue to feed the existing guilt-driven behavior with more of the same, compounding your guilt rather than repenting of the first wrong behavior. Now your second state is worse than your first. In the first wrong, your temptation led you out of your life flow and into a pit. Ignoring your conscience caused you to burrow even deeper.

The pain your conscience creates from wrong choices is a cry to God. If you do not honor it through repentance, something else will come along to alleviate your pain and sorrow, which may come in the form of alcohol, drugs, illicit sex or petty crimes. While these little respites work temporarily, one way or the other, you've just added more guilt to the existing guilt farm you're running. If not checked soon, you're heading for disaster of epic proportions. You've created a cycle of guilt where poor choices on top of poor choices, with *added* poor choices, perpetuate this insanity. Choosing behavior that you know ahead of time will cause you to feel bad afterward, is insanity, whatever the behavior may be. If you continue the madness, after awhile it will begin to run on automatic, and you will become a prisoner within yourself. Again, as guilt is caused by wrong choices, *compound guilt* comes from ignoring the correction and continuing the behavior. Pride supports that system. It is high maintenance, because it takes a tremendous amount of effort to circumvent your conscience. You cannot sustain separation or distraction from it for long. Whenever or whatever your escape is, when it wears off, there are, conflict and all.

Plans abound to evade this marvelous system called conscience, but they are all in vain, because the conscience is brilliant. It *never* fails to whisper to you when you're considering wrong behavior. It gently cautions you, yet will never stop you from making your own choice. It allows you to have your way, but not without warning. You may try to drown it out by putting yourself into a stupor with alcohol, drugs, excess sleep, sex, obsessions and distractions of every kind, but the moment you come back, there it is. You may immerse yourself in passions of every kind, excessive reading, talking, working, even *good* works, *good* deeds, *good* thoughts, food, fun, busyness, pleasures, friendships, family, companionships and traveling, all to quiet the voice of your conscience and keep you in a state of compensation, away from yourself. But it will not let you hide, escape, or silence it for long, because it knows everything you know, and it knows that you know it. You may hide from it in crowds or lose yourself in mobs where you have company in your wrong. There, because the safety of the majority is with you, you say *I have escaped it here...I am safe.* But even in the noise of the crowd, you are alone with your conscience, and it speaks louder than ever, reminding you that you are an individual.

You may continue with distractions of every form and variety known to man, but whatever you do and wherever you go, your conscience goes with you, prompting you toward the good, nudging you toward the right way, and warning you against the wrong. You look for an escape in sleep, and it speaks to you when you awaken. You go through your day and it goes with you, whispering and nudging, still speaking when your head is again upon your pillow. My friend, this will continue nonstop all the days of your life, up to and including the last breath you exhale. Go toward your inner parts, make friends with your conscience, for it is your most faithful friend. It is that friend who is closer than a brother; that friend who will never leave you nor forsake you; that friend who will always lead you toward truth and never lie to you. Learn to listen to, and obey it, and to trust and honor it above all else. Let your individuality be shown to you...it will prevent you from adopting the opinion of the crowd! Be wary of being found on the wide road with all those that travel there. Let your conscience be your guide. You will not be sorry, now or in time to come. The One who designed this brilliant compass and placed it within you, awaits.

Girl Pearl: Those who always speak well of women do not know them sufficiently; those who always speak ill of them do not know them at all. - Guillaume Pigault-Lebrun.

Being an Unwed Parent

It is not easy to raise children. It's a huge long-term commitment, that is not just about feeding them! They'll want what you didn't get enough of, which is to be lavished with love and attention. Both parents bring value to this arena, and there is no downside to a child having all he or she can drink or eat of love while growing up. Human beings have needs, that when they are not met, cause them to become dysfunctional. We also become the walking wounded, wandering around in search of something we are missing. Often we marry (for the wrong reasons) to complete the cycle of what we didn't receive as a child. It is important to note that marriage should be for the right reasons and not because you are needy and wanting. The unwed mother suffers the most. There can be a stigma attached to this experience and there is definitely a predator factor. Men sense when a woman is needy or wanting and act accordingly. Nature does the same. When predators chase a herd of prey, they're looking to weed out and expose the weak, slow, injured, sick, and young. A woman who is needy or in desperate straights, in a given moment may be willing to trade her loneliness for sex, or what she thinks is love. Having a child, naturally makes you into a better person. Having a child out-of-wedlock, *forces* you into becoming a better person. Now, wouldn't you rather become better willingly, under the right circumstances, than be forced under the pains of necessity? It is the difference between making love and being raped.

If you've found yourself in this predicament, you'll need the help of your parents, friends and family to sustain you, and must conduct yourself in such a way that your child's needs come before yours. Sorry, if you have a child, then your work has been assigned to you. By being responsible, making an honest effort and committing to what is right, you'll command help from higher forces, and attract a happy ending to your circumstances. Remember, we are accountable to the One who sent us here, to ourselves and then to our fellow man. We are not animals, and cannot expect to be rewarded as human beings and children of God, when we're acting out animal behaviors.

126

You have to choose a side, girls. Whatever happens, anything can be turned to good when one wishes it so. Wish it so.

Girl Pearl: The woman is so hard upon the woman.

- *Tennyson*

Don't Resent...It Was Never Meant

Resentment is widespread and is a common malady of mankind. It spares no one and damages everyone equally when engaged. Please do not be quick to dismiss this subject. Take a moment, and you will see there is resentment in you, whether it's at the surface where everyone can see, or deep inside you and difficult even for you to see. It's there. When you discover it, it's nothing to be ashamed of, or to hide. On the contrary, be grateful it was revealed to you. If you are willing to look inward and observe yourself, as well as receive feedback and input without laying blame on others, even more will be revealed. The secret is to be still, listen and observe.

One of the roots related to resentment is explained in this way: "something compelling a person to live twice, or return to, or to live something over again." When the same subjects keep coming up for you, then you may want to consider that when you are carrying resentment, there will be the nagging sense of something wrong, or incomplete, in everything you do. It may have been hidden in you since childhood without you being consciously aware of it. Remember, we came into the world innocent. You were not born with resentment. This is a learned, programmed behavior or trauma, and can be unlearned (or let go of) when you are ready to do so. It can be so ingrained in you, that like hypnosis, you perceive that everything wrong is coming from outside you. The symptoms of this are that you will be quick to point out and even create problems where they do not exist. This behavior

127

allows you to play the poisoned part, the *dysfunctional* role that you've been taught and have accepted to play. This is the *how and why* of this intruder. **Resentment is the binding force that keeps any dysfunction active and operating**. How does it come? Somewhere in your life, injustice, trauma, or an event took place that went badly for you and left you injured. Your innocence was tried, pried, loosened, then stolen, leaving behind a bitter memory, kept alive by your judgment of what took place. Your judgment may have been correct concerning what happened, but now you are expressing it through resentment. You have every right to express the wrong, but not to play God by sentencing the offender. Realize there was an intrusion, a trauma that affected your inner child, penetrated deeply, and caused you damage. Realize also, that there was not much you could do about it at the time or you would have. You survived it, and you've been led to this moment. Your focus now is to expose this intruder within you and stop resenting the episode that created and locked it in. By doing so, you free yourself. The unrepentant perpetrator will receive perfect justice, and you no longer have the burden of playing God by judging and sentencing. Who would want the weight of such a burden? Between now and the end, everyone will get what they deserve, and of this you may be certain. The soul is structured so that wrong choices produce guilt. There is no escape from error until true repentance is sought and found. Meanwhile, the person who carries the guilt suffers the most. It's hard to believe, but being in a state of unrest, and having little or no joy, is a very effective punishment. The Lord saw to that and to the solution also.

So what to do about resentment? First, don't run from it, hide it, add to it, or take away from it, but expose it to as much light and reality as you possibly can. God's truth will judge it and send it on its way if you let it. I want you to be free, innocent, whole, and well, starting right now, and letting go of resentment is the first step in the process. Keeping it, on the other hand, will not only damage your health and well-being, but will lead you to make choices based on resentment's dynamics, namely, you will attract, in perfect strangers and would-be suitors, the very things you hate. This is why men and women often choose a mate who exhibits the behaviors of one of their parents. It allows them to continue their resentment, projecting it upon someone else, though they aren't consciously aware of it.

Girl Pearl: *Consider that the purpose of a woman's inner and outer beauty is to attract the best man available. Develop the inner beauty first, and the outer appears more naturally attractive.*

Repentance

God, in all his wisdom, who knows all things, has included in his system a way to straighten yourself out and come back, start over, and begin again, as if it were your first time out. If you have error, blemish or stain of any kind or sort, there is a way back to your innocence. It is called repentance. It is the gift of God, and the first step toward setting yourself toward correction, then redemption. What is repentance? In the Greek, it means: *change*. This is what the guy in the wilderness (John the Baptizer) was yelling at the top of his lungs: *change!* Fascinating thought. We are being told to change. Change what? *Everything* is the answer. People who tried everything but were getting nowhere, sought out this simple truth and found what they were looking for...a fresh start. The procedure was simple. Look at yourself, see your error, be sorry for who you are, what you're doing, and what you're becoming by doing it, then stop what causes those results, go your way and do not repeat it. Do this with everything, and you will have life more abundantly.

Your fallen nature, that which was birthed out of the curse, must die. The process will take time, and begins with you stopping what you are doing, especially if it is not working for you. Therefore, shut down, practice being still, observe yourself while doing it without being willful about anything you see, and allow your fallen nature to start the weakening process. When it

129

does, your true nature will begin to surface and present itself little by little, becoming stronger as you go toward it and listen to it. Full time reflection on your conduct is necessary. Mentally, emotionally, physically, psychologically and spiritually, adjustments will need to be made as your fallen self is revealed. *You* won't have to do much yourself, however. In fact, the hard part is doing nothing, correctly. Just accept what you see and if it is wrong, repent of it and do it no more. The right way to proceed will present itself in due time. Minor changes will come to you in glimpses and meanings throughout your day, should you make it this far. Staying out of your thoughts, not engaging your emotions, and using your five senses wisely, allows God to return to his rightful place as shepherd of your spirit and soul. In effect, he is preparing a place inside you, so he'll be able to dwell with you intimately. But, he cannot move into a tarnished or willful temple. It must meet *his* standards, not yours.

To receive the promises of God and a life beyond the one you dream about, you have some emptying out to do. It will take time, and could take all your life. It will involve pain, discomfort and a pseudo death. You are an eternal being, so there is no risk of you perishing, but there is great risk of your runaway ego, its defense mechanisms, and your five senses all becoming considerably reduced. They must give up the place of having ruled you thus far, and make way for something greater to enter in and expand. That *something* must take its rightful place if you are to travel into eternity. Your false self will not cooperate, but be of good cheer, because it cannot stop you, either.

Many of you have had poor childhood experiences, or not-so-lovely prior relationships. If not properly handled, those experiences become unwelcomed baggage, and wherever you go, they go with you. They interfere and weigh you down as you attempt to recover and start anew. So, before you can begin again, you must be rid of this baggage. Who amongst us has not made a mistake, boo-boo, error, misjudgment, and wrong choice? I am first in line to answer this question. Countless times I bungled and blundered, and was given many chances to make good. Thank God for the system that allows us to recover from a fall. If you answer this question honestly, then you have recognized the need for someone to have come into this world, whose ministry was to save us from this defect (sin). You are on the right track to discover your destiny, purpose, and the mysteries that lead to the kingdom of heaven. All who can relate, who have *been there and done that,* will instantly recognize the truth and be allowed to start anew.

There are dark, invisible forces in the world that have been here long before we got here. Hollywood makes movies on this theme, it is recorded generously in ancient manuscripts, and even by word of mouth in some parts of the world. As you begin waking out of your spiritual sleep, or false existence, and into reality and awareness, these forces will begin to take you seriously, but cannot stop you. When a human being cries out with all the heart, and gives *all* toward wanting to do right and stop the wrong, if motives are pure, God's promises will be activated, because they are *just that*...promises. The same God who gave them will also keep them. To date, there is not a creature or a report in existence that can testify that God does not keep his word. Remember, he is the source of all that is holy, good, truthful, kind and decent, and the list of his purity is endless. He cannot sin, nor can he speak against himself. Consider that he also allows others, including those dark forces, to speak their truths, as truth is what binds the Universe. With this in mind, no creature ever created has been able to use truth to expose a lie against God, because he never lies. This means all the promises you read about are true, and are there waiting for you to receive them.

As a Jewish man to whom the mysteries of Christ have been revealed, who has found the value, worth and purpose Christianity was built upon (Christ), I can tell you there is a time when you will realize you are *wrong* all across the board. Once you realize this and stop practicing that wrong, you are forgiven and allowed to continue your journey with the understanding that you will not repeat your error. The slate is wiped clean, and you are free of blemish or stain. I believe this with all my heart. Not only that, but I have tested the repentance

131

system first hand many times, and it works just as represented by John the Baptizer and Jesus the Christ. In this world and this life, when a second chance (or hundredth) is coveted by those who need it most, what more could anyone ask? Did not Jesus say, *"Go and sin no more?"* What it translates to is a fresh start. A new beginning with a new understanding. This is one of the beauties of life, that as long as you live, you will always have an opportunity for change and betterment.

That being said, if you had a rough start or a hard go of it, if you made poor choices and are living the consequences of them now, then stop this behavior, be sorry for it, and begin anew. Whatever mess you are in will start to clear itself up. Be aware of a very subtle difference in the dynamics of being sorry. There is a sorrow that comes because of a wrong deed, and there is a sorrow of being *caught* in the deed. The first brings remorse and repentance, the second is shallow. Don't confuse the two. How often do you find yourself saying: *I'm sorry*, and not truly meaning it? There are times when an apology is required and sincere, and there are times we use a false *sorry* to defuse an awkward situation by mouthing a few simple words. In other words, we are sorry for the wrong reasons. This not only keeps you from true *change*, but appeases others by using meaningless words. It allows you to argue: *I said I was sorry, what more do you want?* While you may win in the moment, you've lost in the game of life. Why? Because lack of change keeps you repeating your error over and over, and this gives way to the practice and definition of insanity. Then, you wonder why nothing goes well or right for you. You are practicing insanity, but cannot see it.

Judges, police and probation officers, and social workers hear false sorrys all the time. They know it's not real, and have to look beneath the sounds and expressions of false demeanor. Husbands and wives use the easy way out for a multitude of reasons. Perhaps a woman doesn't want to add confrontation to the existing problem. The man wants access to the woman like a bee after the honey, and knows the quick fix of *I'm sorry* may do the trick. One bought time, the other avoided confrontation, but neither got resolution, and the problem still awaits. The fruit of your tree either convicts or exonerates you. True *sorry* at work goes like this: a person realizes his wrong and becomes, for the moment, a person of sorrow and shame. There is a change in behavior and attitude which may even produce a deep sobbing and weeping as the soul expresses its remorse. It is genuine to behold. That which is genuine is also effective, and causes others to recognize the truth as it sets everyone free...free to move on.

When a false *sorry* is pointed out to someone, anger often ensues, thereby proving the point. The system of repentance will be necessary for as long as there is wrong in the world, in any person or deed. It is an affair of the heart and soul, and those that make use of it, exposing themselves in sincere and open repentance, are never the same. Next time you say: *I'm sorry*, realize the power of that statement, and use it for what it was intended to be: a fresh start in a world full of error and never ending issues...a new beginning for you! Don't play with this, but use it wisely and discover the bonus God built into the system. It is called humility. When you are wrong, say so. Humility, when practiced, is quite beautiful in a human being.

Girl Pearl: In this world, when love or beauty are described, a woman is usually nearby.

Girl Pearl: Shyness and modesty are like a double edged sword. Too shy, no guy. Too modest, no hottest. Both are excellent to have, but we must learn how to apply them.

IV. DATING

Companionship

Love, fellowship, and all the benefits of a companion are, and will always be, available. What we do not want are answers to our programming or selfish desires. Programming influences us to choose what we think we need to satisfy a want. Our perceived needs are not really our true needs, but learned behavior responses which prompt us to follow a compulsion of choosing someone hypnotically rather than spiritually (two different worlds and dynamics). Selfish desires are what make us feel good first, then everything else second. Ponder Adam prior to receiving Eve. He did not know what he wanted, nor could he have put it into words, because it didn't exist in his mind. But he sure recognized it when he saw it, and there was nothing in his mind to confuse him on what he saw. So it is with you. God knows what you want.

Now, fast-forward to the present. You may know what you want, but not how to go about getting it. What then? First, unlearn and detach from what you have known and have had (your way). Empty out and find out who you really are. Begin the process of discarding the needy, unattractive aspects of yourself so that something pure and lovely can awaken in you. At the same time, your Prince Charming will begin making his way toward you. Your right motives trigger the process. In the absence of this, you will just return to your habits and programming, and join others in the quest of not knowing, but experimenting as they go. This can be discouraging and damaging. Adjust your motives, detach and refresh, then, as a flower blooms, the honeybee answers the scent.

Girl Pearl: *Love gives nothing but itself and takes nothing for itself. Oh, generous love, make your way toward me...*

Serious Dating Takes Time

Adam's one and only first date was chosen by God and was perfect in every way. Today, having to do the choosing on your own is daunting. Heartache and heartbreak can be reduced by how you start out on this subject, as well as how you conduct yourself as you journey. If you have never dated, have dated unsuccessfully, or have dated recently, then some pointers here will give you a new and effective approach on this subject. For those of you who have had a bad start (or two, or ?) you can now start over again, correctly.

The dating startup process can be considered one of the most dishonest times in anyone's life. In wanting to impress each other, both parties show their best sides, are on their best behaviors, and demonstrate good manners and courtesies. Yet, there is much more going on inside of us all than what we are selling or telling during these initial stages. I am all for showing your best side, making a good first impression, and putting your best foot forward, but we would do well to use first impressions to our good, then get past them to where we really live and who we really are. You see, unless a person knows and loves *all* of you, it may not work out in the long run. Learning about each other will not only take time, but requires skill and heightened awareness. Remember, this process could lead to the most important decision of your life.

If, ultimately it doesn't lead to marriage, then you must learn to navigate through the breakup without getting harmed, while gathering all you can from the experience. There is work to be done. As a woman, you're not only by nature more down to earth than a man via your intuition and emotions, but as an instinctive nurturer, you feel your emotional injuries deeply. When you are hurt, you hurt badly. Therefore, it is oftentimes more difficult for a woman to recover from a failed relationship than it is for a man. Many men are shocked to find out what most women already know. That is, that the woman is in charge during the dating, waiting and courting period....

......she makes her final decisions, and when she is good and ready, and not a moment before, she chooses the man.

Ani-males, the world, dark forces, and your own doubts will try to convince you otherwise. As human beings, of course, men and women are similar, yet we are still in two very distinct sub-categories, each created to work together and compliment the other, while remaining separate. Both were intentionally created to feel and perceive uniquely, to respond differently to their surroundings and to each other, yet still be able to become one in the process. Learning about and understanding these beautiful, complimentary differences between us is essential if we are to experience harmonious relationships.

Girl Pearl: Disguise our bondage as we will,
'Tis woman, woman rules us still. - Moore

The Man May Not Know Either

It may take some pressure off you to know that the guy isn't entirely sure of what's going on in the world of dating. From a man's perspective, the question of how to interact with a woman, while remaining a familiar subject, is confusing to him as well. When a man exhibits signs of awkwardness or periods of silence, coupled with failure to respond or communicate, he may just be trying to figure things out as he goes. No one has been here before. Make allowances for that, withhold judgment of him, and realize he is unfolding to life much in the same way you are. I cannot emphasize enough, that as you are learning to navigate correctly, slowing down in this area of life will benefit you. Guys are eager to learn and explore too. I want you to know how to move forward in some of those unknown and undiscovered territories. Girls, you may find yourselves having to take the lead in training the man to respond until he figures things out. By *training* I do not mean *mothering,* but instructing, guiding, and teaching him about *you.* Remember, he may know about women or girls in general, but he does not know about you. Therefore, it is vital to mine for gold in this arena, and to prolong the dating and courting rituals.

When you come to understand someone, you stop judging them. How do you come to understand someone? By exposing more of yourself and creating a comfortable environment for another to begin opening up. Asking questions, sharing, listening, exploring and inquiring, all help to further this along.

Girl Pearl: I know the nature of women. When you will, they will not; when you will not, they come of their own accord.
- *Terence Eunuchus*

Being Hard to Get

Let's talk about hard to get. Remember, gold acquires its worth by the sacrifice it takes to obtain it. If it were easy to get, it would have little or no value. So it is with you and the dating and waiting scene. Making yourself known, but not available, to every Tom, Dick or Harry is more rewarding and self-satisfying than making yourself available to everyone, but not really being known in the right way by anyone. Famous and wealthy people understand this phenomenon quite well. How do they find anyone who really loves them and not their money, fame, power or public relations and advertising campaign? Not lending yourself to every opportunity that comes your way, but choosing wisely enhances your value and sense of worth. In this process you will develop character through the practicing of restraint and proper care of yourself, and a good man will take notice of that right away. This is not to be confused with being stuck-up, snobby, or arrogant. No, not…not…not. Rather, the message you give to the world is that you've put a high premium on yourself, and the man who wants you will gladly pay the premium. A woman who is confident, caring, aware, well-mannered, clean, and well dressed says a lot, is worth a lot and will get a lot. Be that woman.

Girl Pearl: *He is a fool who thinks by force or skill*
To turn the current of a woman's will.

- *Sir Samuel Tuke*

Say What You Mean

When two people meet, it can be awkward, strange, embarrassing, challenging, stressful, exciting, adventurous, mysterious, and hard work. When we are caught up in the moment, sometimes our emotions take over and we experience an inability to express ourselves efficiently or effectively. This

138

is a paradox worth pursuing, because in the very arena where all this discomfort and challenge takes place, also lies the payoff and reward for participating in it. Go toward it. You are like a bullfighter entering the bullring. In the arena, you may take a licking, but at the same time you are learning to fight bulls. With effort, skill and time invested, eventually you will become a matador. So it is with meeting people and dating. You may find yourself laughing your head off at what takes place. If you are not laughing, then perhaps you are too serious and need to take a step back. The first sign of maturity is often the ability to laugh at one's self. In any event, honest communication with the other person is essential. If you are having a good time, say so, and if not, well, this must be expressed too, but in a thoughtful way and with charity (love). If you feel threatened, uncomfortable or want to change something, you must act on your intuition and do it. *Going along to get along* is not recommended, as it promotes harboring a secret life, which is not good. Let whatever comes out of you be genuine. The other person has a right to expect to know where you stand. Keep in mind, the other person may not know what you're feeling unless you mention it. Then, perhaps they'll rise to the occasion and address it. It's a great time to really know someone, but it all starts with you saying what you mean. Here is a chance to practice boundaries, communication, dialogue, manners, courtesies and people skills. Get to it.

Girl Pearl: If we want a love message to be heard, it has to be sent out. To keep a lamp burning, we must keep putting oil in it.

The Mystery of Not Looking

Have you ever thrown something out only to need it shortly afterwards? Well, the opposite of that is true. Have you ever needed something and it was right under your nose all the time? So it is with seeking a mate. Oftentimes, whatever we are looking for is right under our noses, in our own backyards, and within our reaches. Instead of cultivating our eyes and ears to see and hear it, we complicate and distort the procedure by practicing willfulness and impatience. What I am about to tell you is so simple that you may stumble on it. Just realizing, or becoming aware of a need or desire, is the beginning of the journey to introduce you to it. When we add our dimension to it, such as time, doubt or our own willfulness, or when we seek outside assistance from parents, friends, family or church members, finding a mate can take a different twist. Can all of the above make a difference in finding that someone? Sure, but if you rely on outside sources, you will succumb to those rules and may end up with less than what your true portion would have been.

There is no formula for life. It can be lived in many different ways, and there are a multitude of methods to accomplish the same thing. So, we must not stumble on this way or that, but rather the "right" way, which is the one intended for you from the beginning. Any other way is doable, but will pose obstacles and secondhand results that border on the *lesser of two evils* principle. The clichés *let go and let it happen;* or *let go and let God,* hold true. What is yours is yours. Once you give notice you are ready, or when notice is given to you, get out of the way and let it happen. Those that become more aware of what they do, are more apt to attract what they are looking for. God will reveal intimate things to you, and if you practice patience in the process, he will show you what to do about those things.

Girl Pearl: A woman should be a compliment to a man, and when appreciated, becomes a reward to the man and the union. Seek to compliment first, and the reward for both follows.

Where Do I Go to Meet Someone?

One of the most talked about subjects is where do you go to meet someone? Church, family gatherings, with friends? How about through parties and recreational activities? Are you a member of an online dating service, or how about just friends on a social network? All these things work, although some are better than others. First of all, the key is to go out there, wherever "there" is. Be open to whatever comes your way, and be eager to create ways if they don't come fast enough.

The simplest answer I can give is to go anywhere. Everything finds everything else on this planet simply by being involved in the process of seeking and being found. The human being was designed to be a motion machine, so let's activate it and get going. There is no specific watering hole set up to bring about finding your true love. Consider two very specific practices to begin with. One is to begin some of the inner work suggested, and another is to go out there to be found!

People have tried churches, meeting groups, colleges, work, friends, family, cruises, concerts, dances, blind dates, restaurants and the list is endless, really. Be objective about this. People are wherever you go. Meeting them is not a problem. Meeting someone you want to go out with is *still* not a problem. It's meeting the right person for you, and for the right reasons, that escapes us. My personal favorite is college. You will meet hundreds of people who are all trying to better themselves. Everyone is friendly, outgoing and all have things in common right off. Eating or speaking with each other at college is like pre-dating and is free flowing and natural. If you haven't been to college, you are in for a treat. You will meet many interesting people, make lifelong friends, and get a degree too. Please look forward to it. If you have been to college, perhaps some night courses in something you'd like to get certified in, or an advanced degree, would reintroduce you to this most attractive dating pool. Places of learning attract learned people, which is not a bad place to start. Churches also provide an environment which supports a code of moral conduct important in dating.

141

My least favorite place for dating material is bars, nightclubs or local watering holes. I don't like the environment, and you meet a lot of people who not only can't hold their liquor, but need it to even be themselves. Right there something is wrong. A glass of wine, to relax and sip while enjoying someone's company, can be quite nice. But when the drinking shifts into being more important than the person, it becomes a turn off. Irresponsible behavior, false bravado, and acting out your fears while intoxicated just doesn't make sense. Add alcohol breath to all that, and perhaps your sights for dating potentials can be raised up a bit. Also, bars provide opportunistic and seductive environments, promote drinking, and encourage and support immature behaviors that many come to regret afterwards. Oftentimes, they entice the miserable to deeper misery. When it comes to partying and going out, it all ends up being nearly the same experience over and over again. Learn to skip a few and you will find you didn't miss anything. Others will miss you, and wonder *what ever happened to her?* The simple answer is: *she is traveling down a narrower path looking for realness and satisfaction.* Being purpose driven leads to adventure, and adventure leads to your true destiny. Becoming more aware and selective elevates you above the crowd and brings out the spirit of quest in you.

Girl Pearl: We are sealed containers of something bigger than we are. Only when we unseal ourselves, does the journey begin and does love manifest itself. Empty and refill as necessary.

Going Out for Out's Sake

Ladies, if you are going to make the most important decision of your life, which is to consider marrying, you are looking to do this once and do it correctly, so you can pursue the fruits of marriage and all the wonderful discoveries that accompany it. You can have fun doing this if you do it correctly. But perhaps all you want to do is have fun and not consider a serious relationship just yet. Dating and going out with someone can enhance you in many ways. It can be an excellent opportunity to practice your communication skills and apply your talents, or discover what they are. You will notice as you go through life that it is quick and easy to point out what we don't like, but finding what we *do* like takes time. So, going out for fun and exploring what we like, the process of getting it out in the open so you can see it, work with it and refine it, is very beneficial. Meeting people allows us to see and hear ourselves as we identify with others and observe attributes in them that may stir us inwardly. Your observations about others supply endless input and feedback to you about your journey. Be careful not to judge or analyze, but to observe. We all have blindsides which are those parts of us we cannot see or hear, but others can. As you glimpse other people's blindsides, you will also be able to realize your own, which will lead to personal and inner growth.

Whatever reason exists for moving forward, let's proceed with confidence and common sense. Have a list ready of places you want to go. Girls, I will let you in on a little secret. The guy doesn't know where to go. He doesn't want to know either. He wants you to tell him and he will be relieved when you do. Consult your wish list at this point. Ladies, I would just have a ball going down that list. While dating for fun, you have the opportunity to experience people, practice your skills, eat well and watch movies. Do this with class and not with arrogance. Have a heart of charity and be genuine about the experience. Do not give false hope, or lead a person on with the intent of taking advantage by expecting him to pay your way. If serious intent comes up in conversation, you must respond honestly. The guy will want to know if you had a good time and if you want to go out again. If you can say with all honesty that you did, but you know deep in your heart that this is not going anywhere, end it now. Be gracious, be gentle, be firm and be clear, and you will feel very good about yourself. Remember, hearts are fragile, and very easily injured. Having a conversation like this for the first time will feel awkward. You'll be saying something that may be difficult for another person to hear. This discomfort is normal, and comes with the responsibilities of practicing honesty and fairness in these situations. You'll want to experience and feel the pain and awkwardness that come from your saying *no*, or *I enjoyed your company but I don't think we should see each other again*. It will teach you humility and compassion, and define your character. Feel the newness of the experience and go through it with confidence. Do not miss the opportunity to practice grace and honesty. Have fun...responsible fun, and leave each other on a good, but firm note. As a side note, men do not handle rejection very well. It is one of their biggest issues, although some handle it better than others. Knowing this, choose your words wisely, kindly, but firmly.

Girl Pearl: *Find a righteous man and join your star to his. Two right stars make for a very bright sun.*

Who Pays When We Go Out?

That's a great question. First of all, my dear girls, always carry money with you. I emphasize *always.* Fold up a twenty and hide it somewhere on you. You must have your own independence whenever the need to call upon it arises. Money gives you the freedom to say *no, yes,* or *not now,* and provides you additional power to mean it. It also frees you from obligation, which may be the start of many-a-misery. You see, some dates and friendships, where motives are not pure, will try to purchase you, then at the appropriate time, claim you for themselves. Sex, kissing, favors, or current and future commitments may be demanded of you with the assertion they have invested in you, and now want a return on that investment. When you accept something from someone whose motives are not innocent, immediately there is an unspoken expectation of obligation. My dear girls, this must not be so. You can thwart any feeling of obligation via your confidence level and self-worth. You are of great value, and not subject to negotiations.

If you sense in yourself a feeling of obligation arising, simply pay for yourself. Eventually, as you achieve a heightened level of confidence, and *own* what you do or say, this will not be an issue for you, even if he *does* expect something in return. The issue will be with him. You cannot be bought, neither are you for sale, and no amount of money gives a man the right to expect intimacy in return. This he can expect on your wedding night, if and when it comes. If he has such an expectation now, his motives are not pure, and be glad this has been revealed to you.

Apart from any motives of obligation, it is a very attractive quality to see a person who is confident in their actions. It's a very good sign when the man wants to pay. It says a lot about him. Watch carefully *how* he pays. Is he doing it begrudgingly, modestly, with reluctance, expectations, or how about hidden agendas? Is he uncomfortable with it? Does he object or act awkward at this stage? To the man who is genuinely interested in you, money, time, and obstacles are meaningless. His focus will be on wanting to know and be with you. Money, time and energies would just be tools for him to arrange all that. Now there is someone you'll want to know more about: a man who knows what he wants and knows how to go about getting it. By the way, you can tell a lot about a man by how he spends his money or doesn't spend his money. If a man wants something badly enough, and money plays a part in it, he will find a way for his money to go to work. If he doesn't have much money, then he will have to put to work whatever he has to offer. If, however, he has money and won't spend it, then I would be very interested in hearing why, because this could be an indication of the condition of his soul. The subject of money and mankind is very revealing and beneficial.

If you do allow the guy to pay, let it be because you are comfortable about it, not because you are auctioning off favors or being swayed by money, gifts, or attention. You are worth all that without having to return it. The pleasure of a woman's company, a true, whole woman, is beyond value and compare. It is most coveted, and is reward enough. Become that woman, then be prepared for a path to be beaten to your door.

145

To be fair, in the realm of finances and spending money when interacting, if the guy wants to split the dating expenses in getting to know you, this is acceptable. Some handle it better than others. It is an awkward stage of getting to know someone, so be open, honest, and patient about it. Remember, a tradition is at work which states that the guy must pay, and some of today's guys may not want to do that. If he brings this up prior to the actual date, and handles it in a gracious way, this will tell you a lot about him. Do not feel pressured to make this decision to cooperate (in regard to chipping in) in the moment, but pause and consider it. Assess for yourself whether you want to spend money on yourself with this person. If the answer is *yes*, then do it for that reason. Always consider what anyone has to say, without taking or giving offense. What you do with it is your business and your choice.

Girl Pearl: *If ladies be but young and fair,*
They have the gift to know it. - As You Like It

The First Kiss

If there was ever something that came with pleasure and pain (anxiety), this would certainly qualify. The pleasure aspect is obvious, the going about it may be stressful. When to kiss, how often, where and how, all work on someone's psyche long before the actual kiss. The famous "should I kiss on the first date" is, for some, a very big move forward. Some are so fixated by the subject they forget to have a good time in the moment. Discussing these subjects often allows us to become more comfortable with them. Let's apply that here.

Women, kissing applies to all ages and the magic involved is no respecter of persons. It works on everyone. There are those who do not want to encourage this, but may have to deal with it nevertheless. Some like to take this subject head-on when they first meet you and be done with it. Then, they can

146

spend the rest of the evening at ease, having gotten it out of the way. It can be just a quick peck followed by a quick relief for one or both parties. Even if you didn't like it, you are glad it is over with. If you *did* like it, well let's have a nice time.

Cheek Kissing: This is used for greeting and approval of seeing and wanting to be with someone. It can be a *thank you* or *see you again* experience. It can be an excuse not to kiss on the lips, too. People who want to stay in control, can steer the action to the cheek, no problem. A quick jerk of the head quickly instructs the other person where to go. Then, you can pull in or out as necessary. Lips do not actually have to touch anyone's cheek either. You can just go cheek to cheek with or without puckered lips. This communicates quite a bit about both of you. Just be aware of it. It can also set the theme for the evening. Send the message you want sent, girls.

Lip Kissing: I'm referring to the peck with the lips closed. This can be an approval message that says, *I want to see you again* or *I'm glad to see you.* It's a warm and inviting gesture that has the ability to be turned up or down, depending on the message you want to send. I won't go into graphic detail, but there's something about this subject that teaches you everything you need to know in the moment. Some women like to add sound effects like a soft *hmmm* or a gentle touch to the arm during the kiss. It's a message of approval...it says....*let's continue.* Remember ladies, you set the tone and the action. You are in control. Don't surrender that control, but use it to communicate. The first kiss is usually remembered and talked about, so look forward to it, but don't rely too much on it. Learn to trust yourself first, then proceed with confidence on whatever you decide to do. This is just a signal from you to him on how to proceed. For those of you who are professional kissers (experienced), there is still always a first time with anyone you *kiss* for the first time.

Girl Pearl: Look for someone who can help you and will not help themselves to you.

147

Boundaries

There is nothing more attractive on a girl or woman (or more beneficial to her), than establishing how far she will go or allow the guy to go. This applies to the mental, emotional, physical, psychological, and spiritual realms. You must learn to respect yourself, and setting boundaries will help you learn this, while teaching others also. A girl without boundaries is missing value, respect, mystery, adventure, and worth. You start out in life as a prize, wanted by all men. Even if you had parents that didn't love you, that doesn't detract from what I just said. It just means that they missed out on experiencing the one and only you.

Gather yourself up and create for yourself a list of dos and don'ts that are not negotiable. Having this list ahead of time will solidify your own position at the necessary times, and you will prevail. There is great power in this application when used correctly. Let's expand on this farther, and take them one by one:

The Physical Realm: Make sure your *"no"* means something, and be prepared to back it up all the way, if necessary. You may allow yourself to be kissed or not. Touched in areas of your body or not. You call the shots on how someone can approach you and touch you. In addition to your *"no,"* moving away firmly and abruptly sends a clear message. Grabbing or taking someone's hand off of you is appropriate also. You do whatever it takes to get your message across, and do not back down.

The Mental Realm: There are individuals who assault your mind with meaningless chatter or questions that go nowhere. In most cases, they are acting out what has been done to them, and have become unable to stop themselves from engaging in the same behavior. Not realizing it, they do this to others. Recognize a mental assault, and put a stop to it by asking questions: *"Why are you asking me that"* or, *"what is your point?"* If you cannot get a clear answer, simply employ your boundary, and instruct to move on to another subject. You can

148

also change the subject deliberately as a way of taking a stand. Allow only what is acceptable to you. Excusing yourself and walking away is also an option.

The Psychological Realm: This has more to do with your beliefs on certain subject matters. Be careful not to confide, open up to, or make yourself vulnerable to a complete stranger. Trust will come later, and there will be time to venture into this realm when you decide you are ready. Remember, letting others have access to your mind leaves you open to their suggestions. Access to this vulnerability in you must be earned, and you control the rights to it.

The Emotional Realm: This would be you sharing your feelings with someone who you feel comfortable with. It is an intimate arena reserved for the special few who can handle their emotions, then share them accordingly. This boundary must be respected, first by you, then by whomever you allow in.

The Spiritual Realm: Here, one may believe in a Creator or God different than another. There are thousands of world religions, but only one God. Many believe in God, but have differing viewpoints as to who he is. Take Jesus for example. You have over 2000 different Christian religions but only one Jesus. So 1999 of them are wrong and every one of them claims it's the other guy who has it all wrong. It may be wise to limit your sharing on this subject to *yes* or *no* questions and responses, and not go into any detail in early stages. If the guy is a Satan worshipper or doesn't believe in any God; you should promptly bail. Get to really know something about the other person before you tackle such a serious subject.

To sum it all up, unless you establish boundaries as to what is acceptable to discuss and when, you will be subject to assaults in these realms which weaken or cheapen you. You were not put here to be assaulted in any way. It is wise to have a belief in God and hold that thought until you feel comfortable enough to expand on it with someone else. Then, you'll want to either honor the existing belief or increase it. Not respecting this boundary can leave one without a life foundation on which to build, and may result in being swept away by the storms of life.

Girl Pearl: Love is but a gift of sharing your heart with another and being willing to accept part of theirs.

Second Chance Dating

Why not? There are many reasons to give someone another chance after a flopped first date. First off, you'll have experience (maybe not the best one) and familiarity going in your favor, which reduces the anxiety that comes with the unknown. Secondly, practice saying more of what you really mean and what you would like to see happen, then learn from the responses (or experience) or lack of them. Sharpen your skills, making this a learning experience. Practice at what you are doing to become better at it. Realize that you may have missed a few things the first time out also. This is not Hollywood, where everything is rehearsed and then filmed. This is real life, where situations occur and we learn as we go. Furthermore, awkwardness is part of dating and meeting someone, and it doesn't happen the way movies or television present it. I'm speaking of all the outtakes and blunders made by actors and directors that cause them to reshoot a scene. Then, you see the final, perfectly flowing, one to two-hour episode where everything went as planned. Do you actually believe that people talk perfectly, wait for each other to finish speaking, then respond with perfection all while living life? Come on…this is entertainment and rehearsed fantasy. It is based on real life, but is not real life. You are real life.

Keep in mind the dynamics of the famous "learning curve" which is present in anything you do for the first time, or where you're venturing out and exploring. Since you don't know what to expect, you learn from *doing,* and from the mistakes which are part of the learning process. Knowing all this, seeing someone a second time is not only further training for you, but gives him a chance to recover, make good, and refine his learning curve. Who knows, the second time out may surprise you. I know it will surprise him. Now ladies, let's not forget our common sense. If the guy practiced the art of being a first class jerk, need I say more about revisiting with this person? Always remember that you are in charge. Do what you will and have fun doing it.

Girl Pearl: You don't need a man, but having one is not a bad idea.

Shopping for Company

You don't need a man. You must never need anything except to become a better person and be thankful for what you have. You should be whole and complete unto yourself, and if and when you join yourself to a man, it will be to compliment you and enhance your life experience. He will want the same. If you think having a man will complete you and make you whole, you are not ready to become a good companion. This is an unresolved issue that must surface and be dealt with before going into the dating circuit with serious intent. Perhaps you can explore it there as well, but the law of attraction cannot be manipulated. Whatever you are putting out, is what you are summoning. Just know that we are looking to upgrade our life experience and perhaps pass on the gene of the future in a loving and intimate way.

As we begin dating, a good comparison to it is shopping. When you go shopping, you don't by the first thing you see. If you do, stop it right now! There is more to shopping than that. If you are not sure, you sample, you may try something on, you ask for feedback or you inquire. On certain items, you stare into a mirror and you are looking for a positive sign, a signal that says *yes* or *no, not yet,* or *I will think about it.* More experienced shoppers refuse to buy the first time around, and even take a time-out to allow their emotions to be removed from the process. This ensures that you end up with what you really want, and not something you bought on impulse, then regretted. This phenomenon is known as *buyer's remorse*.

Now let's see how this applies to dating. In the consumer world, there are laws that protect the shopper against false advertising, and require that food products have detailed ingredients information listed on what is being offered. Not so with human beings. There are no laws requiring a list of ingredients or prohibiting false advertising. You don't know what you're getting, and you can't always believe his sales approach. He may look, sound, and act like a good catch, but lurking inside may be things you will not like, or may even loath at a later time. Not everyone in the dating marketplace is wholesome and playing by the same rules. Another point to consider, which is common during a shopping spree, is that people buy from people first, then the product (whatever you're selling) catches their interest. They become more interested in what you're selling if they like you first...

...and so it is in the dating world. If you are likeable, inviting, approachable, non-threatening and sincere, you may notice a little path leading up to your door from people wanting to come to you. If you want a guarantee on how to attract people, learn to be a good listener, and you will be mobbed. Operate on the principles of your word being good enough. By that I mean, when you speak, mean what you say. When you do, you will find people being very attentive to what comes out of you, because they'll find you to be credible. Do your share of talking, and connect until you are both reading "go" signals. Acting in a disingenuous way produces less than desired responses. To taint that process with insincerity, dishonesty, and false hope, while pretending to do otherwise, violates a person's being. It also cheapens you. Don't do this even though it is easy to do. *Keep it real,* as they say.

Some of the online dating services require submission of detailed questionnaires, designed to offer as much data as possible for others to make informed decisions. This business approach may be cute and functional, but the desires of the heart remain unknown, and more importantly, untested. It holds true in the retail industry, that when you buy something it should work as presented, or all bets are off. Some people who use dating services may be trying to get lucky by shortening the process to begin enjoying the rewards. The very act of hiring an agency may be interpreted as starting out on the wrong foot, simply because it reeks of willfulness. Please keep in mind that the business of people is the business of people, and people are everywhere. Learning how to mine for gold where you are, makes you richer for the experience. What you are looking for is not quite out there as you may think. In fact, it is *closer* than you may think, and becoming aware helps you see more clearly. In the dating arena, a less intellectual, functional business-type approach is recommended. Many cultures employ the business tactic, with mixed results. Reverse this thinking. Lengthen the process and put off the obvious rewards until you know, understand, and accept the person for the right reasons and motives. Again, learn to open your heart and not your mind in regard to this subject matter.

There is something called fool's gold which looks, feels and seems like real gold, only it isn't. It got its name for two reasons: First, it fools you into believing it's something it's not; and second, if you do believe it, you have become a fool. Not everything that glitters is gold, and people today glitter, squeak and squawk all the right noises and make all the right moves, but are not truly what they are representing themselves to be. Time and testing will bring this to the surface. No fool's gold for you!

Girl Pearl: *Often the sign for needing to get to know someone better is the fact that you don't like them when you first meet them.*

Paternal, Maternal or Trauma

The two greatest dynamics built deeply within every human being are: *everyone wants to be loved, and no one wants to be alone.* Men and women everywhere are in the never-ending process of seeking to fulfill these two dynamics for themselves, attempting to accomplish *being loved* and *not being alone* correctly, and yet it does not fare well for our species in most cases. You see, if you are moving under a compulsion instead of being led from within, your seeking may be for the wrong reasons. We must examine our motives to see what we are seeking and why. It is one thing to go shopping on a full stomach, and another to go shopping while hungry. On a full stomach, you buy less. On an empty stomach, you buy more.

When it comes to the subject of a lifetime companion, you should not go shopping while you are hungry, needy, or wanting, lest the wrong in you attracts the wrong in someone else, and you settle for whatever comes along first. Be aware that we tend to choose or gravitate toward what is familiar to us.

Judgment or contempt for either parent can infect you with the same behavior, or nature, that you so dislike. You may unwittingly be under that influence and seek to replicate it through marriage and relationships. Both negative and positive forces can become familiar to us. How you relate to your family can affect how you will choose or perceive someone else.

Your childhood is a great place to revisit and explore. It is a treasure trove of data waiting to be accessed by you. Nearly all your answers, as to why you do or think the way you do, can be found there. In some cases people marry to continue the hate process they had with one parent or another. A man who resents his mother, for instance, may seek out a woman who would be a suitable candidate to continue the hate process with. This is not the man you want to start your dating and courting process with, dear girl! Those dysfunctional and dark forces are in operation all over the earth. I am setting you up to succeed, and for the dark forces to fail. They would wish it otherwise, but not on my watch. Not on your watch either.

Paternal: It is well known that women who hate or resent their father figure, will oftentimes seek out that experience *for better or for worse*, and it turns out mostly *worse*. Sometimes we seek things out in order to return to the episode that traumatized us, so we can relive it with a better ending (so we think) and be made whole. Other times we revisit those traumas to recapture either the virtues that were lost in the lesson of that moment, or something we didn't have or get at the time. The most damaging reason, however, is the attempt to keep that hate alive because we have grown used to it, and this false life and its sustenance is all we know. Knowing yourself is the key to preventing you from duplicating the trauma you grew up with. Get rid of the resentment and programming before going out there into the dating realm. To begin the procedure of becoming free of resentment and hate, you must first realize it exists, that you are doing it, that it's wrong, and its continuation is dysfunctional. (See Repentance chapter for more detail.) Remember girls, you want to attract someone for the right reasons. For righteousness sake.

Maternal: Seeking out a weak man, or one that is more feminine in nature, may be you looking for mom (in him) to either find what you didn't have, or to keep the hate alive for the mother you did have. It is very convenient to have someone to hate that close to you. So, you marry him. Instant hate when you need it. Of course, he married a woman that berates and weakens him just like his mother did. Both are unhappily married thinking the other is crazy. What you must realize is that neither one of you is your true self. Ladies, we need to take a deeper look at this.

Trauma: Injustice, excessive punishment, neglect, tyrannical behavior, being dominated and manipulated, tricked, deceived, or mistreated all play on us when we are growing up. These things rob you of your childhood. They will continue to rob you all the way to your grave, if you let them. *Resentment* is the unholy pit bull that locks you into these episodes and binds you to dark forces. It has a way of setting you up, either to conform or rebel to what has happened. You see, you either accept (conform) and go along, or you reject (rebel), but in either instance, you are still not yourself and continue to be influenced by your circumstances. What you didn't realize is there is a third choice, your *true* choice. Why conform or rebel? Reject both, and realize you do not know what to do, and begin the process of wanting to know. God will honor this journey and even commands you to activate it in this way. Be still and let things be submitted to you while you observe. He knows eventually it will lead to him and from there, all the right choices follow. By forgiving the injustice and dropping the judgment that comes with it, we free ourselves to become closer to our truer selves. You may be drawn to your personal traumas if you have been exposed to *conform or rebel* dynamics, and seek them out as the only life you know, or because you have the need to continue to hate by perpetuating it. Neither is the real way, and you need to get whole and let the baggage go.

You must wonder what it would be like, and what *you* would be like if you were seeking someone for the right reasons. To seek with an open heart and receive an open heart in return, is not only possible, it is extremely satisfying. Then, to the business of testing the love for its purity and honoring that love when it stands up to the test. That's what we are going to do, and from this moment on, while there is breath in your body and a desire to better yourself, you shall.

Girl Pearl: Of all wild beasts on earth or in sea, the greatest is a woman. - Menander

The World of Men

From all his glory and intended glory, Adam, out of disobedience, fell and came under a curse, which is the current condition of man. He reverted to a lesser life form, an animal state of existence, closer to the males of the animal kingdom, and farther from his true kingdom, which was heaven. He must sweat for his bread and labor for his wants, not unlike a mule or an ox. Truly, the mighty have fallen. Now, the animal man must rise above his cursed nature and find his way back, using grace and the mercy of God. Jesus shows you how to do this successfully.

True men play a tremendous role and have great responsibility on this planet. Look around you and at our history. Man has failed to steward himself, his family, and the world, and neither God, women, nor the world, are happy with it. Now, males must rise up again and become men to win back favor with God and everyone else. Until they do, they remain males, and in this state, perpetuate and support the misery that plagues the planet and its past. However, that can be changed thanks to God's plan of redemption, and males, via repentance, yearning to return to their once rich heritage as stewards of all the earth, can become true men and sons of God. Until that happens in a man, dear girls, *males* will not satisfy your heart's desires. If you want a long-term, rewarding relationship, where

157

the promises of God made to man will overflow from him to you, then you must await or awaken the true man.

Men have a duty to the world, communities, families and each other to maintain the standard of being a man. When this is properly practiced and carried out, order and predictable results flow freely, and everyone prospers. God can be God, man can be man, and woman can truly be woman. Males, or weak men, lean toward the more animalistic behaviors that lack virtue and character. Unfortunately, there are an abundance of males in today's society. Some of his attributes are: he is not vigilant for himself, his family, or his associates. He may shame his wife or companion in public. In private, one must do what his heart instructs him to do, using charity liberally in making his points. But in public, to shame another person made in the image of God....pause here. This is not the work of a man. The weak man is a friend to his children rather than a father. He chooses the path of least resistance, using the children, no less. Another characteristic often accompanying the weak man is that he gets drunk. This man is neither a hero, a role model, nor someone you can trust. The weak man does not keep the commitment *'til death do you part,* and also betrays what is right, fair, true, decent, honorable, and just. This is not allowed ever, even unto death. Men who are abusive, angry, controlling, will not listen to reason, and are not ready to learn or progress, are attributes of the weak man. Pass these men by, nay, drop them like a hot brick, as they have some hard lessons to learn. Any man who is a flirt, particularly when he is with you, is a potential womanizer, and I recommend extreme caution, because that man is heading for a fall. Avoid these types of men like the plague, because if you don't, they will plague you in the end. These behaviors are not natural, and if the potential duet is to succeed and deliver the promises of God to each other, the dysfunctions must go. A man without character is not ready to take on the responsibilities of a wife, the world, children, a job, and other men.

Girl Pearl*: Stand on solid principles and your portion will come to you. It is one of the laws of the Universe.*

What Guys Say to Other Guys

Ladies, the word on who you are gets out pretty quickly. That word comes from you and your behavior, and you can do with it as you like. Being known for *not* being sexually active is being famous for the right reasons. Being known for being promiscuous is famous for the wrong reasons. Men key into *either* fame and quickly respond to it. The girl who guards her secrets and guards them well, has an allure that is most attractive to all. Ani-males will be attracted to you for selfish reasons, and may even see you as a challenge. You will have to weed them out. Promiscuity, the infamous one, becomes a hot ticket into the ani-male kingdom...where someone buys you short-term, with long-term consequences for you.

I have heard men describe women in ways where I had to leave the room or, in some cases, address the men who were commenting by letting them know they were out of line. It can be vile and degrading. When men talk disparagingly about women, it calls to my mind that those women were once little girls who lost their way. Don't lose your way, and if you did, come back now. You set the standards for yourself, so set them high if you want to find a good man. The ones that want to know you for the wrong reasons...I ask you...what is in it for you? Guys tire quickly of having their way with a girl who allows them, then they'll treat you accordingly. Letting yourself be used in return for a good time is a bad deal. It will be just a matter of time before you'll find yourself alone again, wounded, and used for the experience. Realize that if you do not correct this behavior, a woman has her prime and her time, and it comes and goes quickly. Don't use it up unwisely. Weak men or males look for two kinds of women: those they want to have fun with, and those they want to marry. Decide now for yourself what is important to you, who you want to be, and what you want to be known for. No man brags about the woman everyone "had" and how he married her. Sorry Girls. The one he "had" and the one who "got away," both become famous stories to tell around. They falsely benefit by boasting how they are real men, and have fun telling *both* stories for their own amusement. In reality, they are not real men, and this is not a subject to boast

159

about or make fun of. Some men will not deny sowing their wild oats, but will tell you that when they were good and ready, they married the best one out there. You will benefit more by being the one that got away. Know this now. What is the difference between the one who got away and the one who didn't? Self-respect and lack thereof. You must put a high premium on yourself, and you cannot purchase self-respect. It has to be cultivated and maintained, and that comes about, in large part, from making the right choices. Dear girls, you will reap what you sow. Unwanted pregnancies, resentment for men, and a permanent bitterness in your life can all be avoided if you abstain from the pressures of sex before your time. Pressures to conform and be carried away from your true self will be presented to you constantly. Make up your mind early and hold fast. Do this work, set your boundaries, know who you are and be ready to stand for what you believe before making yourself available to the dating public. When you are sure, begin the process, then you can refine and evolve your systems as you go. Your morals, wants, dislikes, and the ability to communicate them must be up and running if you are to attract a decent person. If not, you attract another type. Remember the rule: if you want a good friend, you must be a good friend. If you want a decent experience, you must offer one too. You attract whatever you take a stand on. Always choose the solid rock and sure foundation. You see, as you venture out, your beliefs will surely be tested. If you have built on solid principles, all else will crumble, come and go, but you will go on. The minute you allow someone else have access to your "inner" self inappropriately, you are spending your worth and esteem foolishly. I encourage you to spend it wisely, as it is priceless and mourned over when lost before its time, robbed from you, or spent unwisely.

Girl Pearl: Women were made to be loved. When they don't get it, something is not right. Until that is righted, all remain slighted.

Men Think with Body Parts, Women with Emotions

It is appropriate that I make the following announcement at this time. All men are opportunists when it comes to sex. So strong is the command to be fruitful and multiply when combined with the fallen nature of man, rarely can a man refrain from indulging himself, then possibly regretting it later. When you mix this with a man's ego and pride, males sometimes will say or do anything to conquer a woman and have his way. Left in our wake is a trail of resentment and guilt because motives were all wrong.

Ladies, you must always trust what your inner parts tell you, rather than what your emotions tell you, or what you are being told by a man. Yes, your emotions are real, but so is your intuition, common sense and conscience, and all these work together to serve you. You must listen to your moral compass and not be persuaded otherwise. If you do not know the difference, than take the ultimate cure. First say *no,* and then take a *time-out!* Just take two steps back and you will see for yourself what is going on, and whether it is real. Say *no* and mean it. You have nothing to lose by doing so, even though dark forces will tell you otherwise. At the very least, even males understand that it is not to their advantage to involve themselves in something they cannot win. Why would you? Yours comes at a cost. Spend the best time of your life guarding yourself and your beliefs, and let no one have their way with you. No one.

Now, when a woman is operating at optimum, she tends to be very much in touch, or down to earth. Deep feelings are part of a woman's journey, and they influence her thinking, sometimes to her good and other times to her detriment. Should a woman's feelings line up with her trust and vulnerabilities, her slot machine is poised to hit 777. Ladies, we need to move slowly and not be persuaded otherwise. There must be some space and time between your feelings and your actions for your own sake and safety. On this subject, an ounce of prevention is worth a pound of cure.

Girl Pearl*: Hearts will break and yet, brokenly, they live on.*

Sweet Sounding Words

Sweet sounding words? You deserve more than that. We don't want to receive rewards that are substitutes for the real thing. Some people can take words and make them become just that. Actions have to line up with words, and must pass the tests of being genuine. There are clever people out there, who have learned early in life to make all the right moves, using sweet nothings to make them come alive in you and mean something, all in order to take advantage of you. Oh, it may be pleasant to experience, but how real it is, who can say? Their 'rap' is quite believable and works on most people. Simple, common folk continue be amazed at larger than life scenarios, and smooth talkers always captivate them. Reward fast talking with fast walking.

That means either you walk away or make it clear that words are a small part of what is going on. Words have to mean something and lead to something greater than noises. If all you want is to hear "sweet nothings" and meaningless feel-good statements, that is all you go home with ladies. Nothing.

Online dating sources usually list all the positive strengths and attributes of a person. The majority of the listings are inaccurate, and don't tell the whole story. What are you expecting to find? It sounds positive, and is geared to move you forward, but that doesn't mean it is real. Many men (married too) sign up on these dating services hoping to play the numbers and get lucky. Don't let this happen to you. As I've said before, dating can be one of the most dishonest times in a person's life. Hearing, feeling, and sharing nothing but positives does not address the whole *being* of a person. The whole being wants to be fed, and will demand it, either now or later on. Acknowledge the good manners and courtesies while dating, but at some point you need to dig a little deeper. Being swept off your feet by sweet sounding words is not a whole experience, plus you are entitled to more than that. The phrases *"I love you"* and *"I like you,"* and what people really think of you, are better when demonstrated and acted out, than when spoken.

Girl Pearl: A ship will drift until there's a captain at the helm. Women must take the helm until more help arrives.

The Married Man

There is a creature out there that looks, talks, smells, and quacks like a duck. But it is not a duck. It is a wolf who has learned a few tricks to take advantage of women. It is the married man who is not happy at home and is now on the prowl. Girls, the first thing your common sense should tell you is that this male is not a good catch. If he doesn't honor the one he is already with (or himself), why would he honor you? Women who are desperately lonely, dysfunctional, tired, or vulnerable, fall prey to his charms. This ani-male is persuasive, too. He has the words and the experience to help make you feel complete. He knows how to woo you. He may be good looking and have money, power, and fame. The point is, he is after your body for

163

his pleasure. Another notch on his meaningless belt. When he first meets you, he is already having mental sex with you. He is plotting to turn you into his personal whore. I am sorry to be rude here. Ladies, some of you can tell when a man is looking at you for the wrong reasons. There is no mistaking it. His mouth says otherwise and tries to confuse or confound you, and it all spells doom for you.

Ladies, this type of ani-male has separate emails, phone numbers, and even frequents meeting places of available singles. This predator will have a story that has been refined over time. You see, the first few girls he used it on busted him cold. But then he learned what girls and women wanted to hear. The angel of light (the deceiver) is his mentor and instructor, and he, himself, is a predator and destroyer. He will tell you that if he finds the right person, he will leave his wife in a heartbeat, and his hope is that you will believe him. Of course you'll have to perform for him in order to qualify. Reassuring you that he is separated, not in love, lonely, or in the process of divorce are not acceptable reasons for him to be out there looking, while under the oath of marriage.

Some of the stories you will hear are so made-up and ridiculous, that one should respond to them with a raised eyebrow and quick exit. He is going from one sexual experience to another, and possibly has more than one or two going during the same timeframe. Don't be his next use. A person like this is not using his moral compass, and if you are attracted to him, *your* moral compass is broken. Run as quickly as you can in any direction, and cut this guy off. This is going nowhere real fast.

Girl Pearl: *I've seen your stormy seas and stormy women,*
And pity lovers rather more than seamen.
- Byron

I Will Change Him

It is worthy to point out a huge mistake and blunder made by all your prominent sisters who have gone before you. It is an error and temptation that must be outed and cast away permanently. It starts by you thinking, upon discovery of a negative or unattractive trait or belief in your intended, that you will change him, either now or later on. *I will* change him. Do you see the *willfulness* even in the statement? *I will.* This thought process leads to doom, resentment and instant unhappiness. Consider this a snare and temptation that you must not fall into. It sets into motion dynamics that will cause you to lose in the end. Harry Potter may have the power to change someone, but you do not, and thinking otherwise is *your* defect. Remember what happened when your parents or friends tried to change you? Not a pleasant experience. Even if you attempt it and it seems to have worked for a time, it will not last. The change must come from within a person. To attempt this, you will have built on sand, and will find your current or future union sinking at the first sign of a storm (argument). Hear this again: YOU CANNOT CHANGE ANYONE! Even God gently *submits* information to you all the days of your life. He prompts, nudges, and whispers things for your consideration, hoping you will rise to the occasion and become interested to explore or discover them for yourself. After doing so, he wants you to come to him willingly. It is his *goodness* that draws you toward him. He is never forceful or demanding. He is inviting, patient, instructive and attractive.

Decide early on, when you discover something in a man you are not sure you can live with, that you will either accept it, explore it and continue, or reject it and move on. These are all things that should be worked out during dating and courtship, well before marriage. Marriage will present its own unexpected challenges and surprises, therefore it is wise to reach closure and understanding of as many issues as possible beforehand. The more that comes up during the dating process, the better for you. We already know the divorce rate is high and steady, and is influenced heavily by the process of attempting to change one another. What you see, hear, and experience over time is what you are going to get. Don't travel in a fog. Refuse anything less than the right, true and decent way for yourself. This is not the time for you to play Mother Teresa, or savior, and you must resist becoming an enabler or expecting he will change. If someone is trying to hide these things from you, they will not outlast time or the testing methods I have suggested. You should now be on your way to an awareness journey, learning how to watch, observe, behave and grow as a woman with every passing day and circumstance. You have all your life to figure things out as you learn and progress.

Giving due respect to everyone on this planet, certain behavior is not acceptable, especially when interacting with creations made of sugar and spice and everything nice (that's you, girls). Cursing, lack of manners, infidelity, drugs, drinking, lying, cheating, deceiving, stealing, and any type of abuse including mental, emotional, psychological, spiritual, and physical, is not for you. You will know these things over time, or be lucky enough to see them early on. These dysfunctions cannot be covered up or hidden. They require feeding, and are always out and about seeking what they can devour. Don't let them feed on you. I am not against anyone, personally, who practices these dysfunctions. I'm just against the things they practice. I find them to be very unattractive on any human being, and I don't want that for you. So, please don't take on these kinds of dysfunctions unless you want them and want to become *like* them. To undo dysfunction, trauma, and damage requires hard work and diligence on your part, and a willingness on the other's part to want change, and *that* part is not within your control. In some instances, suffering will be required of the person, as this behavior is unacceptable to the universe, to God, to humanity, and even to the one who carries this abnormal and unnecessary baggage around. Guilt follows them all the days of their lives, rewarding them with *compound* guilt for repeating the behavior, and all this leads to fear, depression, and resentment. Woe to anyone that travels this way.

Girl Pearl: Man was made when Nature was but an apprentice, but woman when she was a skilful mistress of her art. - Cupid's Whirligig

Look for Someone Who Loves Right

Reach for the heights on this, ladies, because you can't go wrong if you look for Mr. Right. By that I mean a person who *loves* right.

Then, you want him to love you in the same way he loves right. This, Mr. Right will do, because he is a man who follows his conscience, and seeks to do what is right. He embraces goodness, justice, decency, fair play and honesty above all things. He is nowhere near perfect, but he strives for it. He may even make more mistakes than others, because he's on a journey, experimenting with life inquisitively, and trying to work things out. He is a man of character. Men who respect their parents, siblings and contribute to the care of their family, will love, protect and provide for them without the asking. In his world, women, children, and the weak receive rest and nurturing first, then himself. He is approachable, flexible, and sensitive to those around him, starting with his wife and children. He cherishes, nurtures, guides, corrects, and directs his wife with all his heart, using patience, attentiveness, and having an understanding of her needs. He recognizes this is his helpmate, his second set of eyes and the holder of his trust, and that he must be to her all things, and she will show him a loyalty that others only dream about. A true man keeps his marriage commitment. He makes an excellent business partner, neighbor, and friend. He keeps his word and his character beyond reproach consistently. He promotes fairness and justice in all his doings, and obeys what is right in his heart no matter what the cost. He has charity (love) in all he does, and finds favor with God. Who amongst you doesn't want to find favor with God and raise a family under that banner? This is a fulfilling and everlasting love for both parties. The foundation cannot be shaken, and not only will it weather all the storms, but it will allow you to continue building on solid ground all the way to the end. If you surrender yourself to an unrighteous man, and build on what he offers, where do you think you'll be headed when the storms begin to hit?

Girl Pearl: *When a man is trying to win a woman's hand, he forgets he must first win her heart.*

Good Stories in the Bible

Throughout the Bible, you will see that God always looks upon the heart of a person to discover truth. When Pharaoh's heart was tested, it was found to be hard. It was said of King David he had a heart after God's. Isaiah pointed out that men praise God with their lips, but their hearts are far from him. These are the kinds of truths we are looking for in ourselves, about everything and anything. We want the truth about ourselves at all costs, and even if it causes us to suffer, we want as much of it as we can stand. It resides in the heart, and we do well to listen to and encourage that structure. When the heart speaks, everyone's needs get met. God wants to increase the truth in every human being. Men examine the hearts of other men, looking to establish trust and assign responsibilities. It is the most favored thing to have, and very much worth pursuing. Let your heart be filled, then emptied all the days of your life. When all the right things flood the heart and create fullness, then it is up to you to empty it out and share this treasure with others. Then, repeat this process as often as you can. When it comes to love, and the affairs of the heart, it is our *hearts* we must open to the subject, and not so much our minds.

Girls, if God finds a man with a good heart and wants to increase it, he can use that man more, and bless him at the same time. If this is happening, you want to be in on it, and you want your children, family and friends to be in on it too. Abraham, Joseph, and Moses, along with other greats in the good book, demonstrate how important it is for a man to be right in his heart with all things as he journeys. That includes you, too, ladies. So, how does this work? The next chapter will answer!

Girl Pearl:
In order to find a true man, one must become a
true woman. Males abound, but true men must be found.
This is accomplished by elevating oneself from female to
woman. He goes from male to man. Eventually, a true man
and a true woman will meet up. So be it.

The Basics

Suppose you are introducing the man you are dating to a special friend or family member. Does he make eye contact? Is there realness in the exchange and genuineness in the moment? Make allowances for awkwardness and the learning curve. Listen and observe without judgment or analysis. No single introduction or experience tells the whole story. So to be fair, you are looking for many of these scenarios in order to gather a healthy experience and insight into the character of this person of interest. This takes time. Ask your friends and family what they thought about the person. What they liked or didn't like. It's called feedback and input. It doesn't mean that what they tell you is what took place. No. It was just their experience and is to be listened to. What you do with it is another thing. Also, we are not seeking anyone's approval. This is a matter for the heart. *Your* heart, that is, and then his. However, there is a familiar saying: "when ten people say you are drunk, go lie down." So dear girls, if the same things keep coming up in the feedback you receive, please take it in. Your emotions may be blinding your heart and common sense. If you remain open to feedback and detached from your emotions, you will not allow them to direct your heart.

Girl Pearl: *O Woman, you are not merely the handiwork of God, but also of men; these are ever endowing you with beauty from their own hearts...You are one-half woman and one-half dream.*
- Rabindranath Tagore

What You May See

Some key things to remember are that no one is perfect and everyone is on a journey of knowledge and discovery. What you are looking for is evidence of a bright nature, an open disposition, intelligence, a humble attitude, and an honest intent.

170

You definitely want someone who is evolving and open to change. Be alert to looking for these things *in the rough* as well. By that, I mean in the pursuit of trying to gain character, people learn as they go. Remember, wanting to better oneself is a strong indication of being open and available to new and good things. There will be mistakes, misunderstandings and errors. However, time will allow for behavior corrections and modifications to take place. People have the ability to assess and make changes when they see the need to do so. Allow for this, and watch for results. You will want to become aware of things you can live with. People are people. What you see, you'll eventually get, if you choose this person. Be prepared to accept some things about him that are not altogether to your liking, just as he will be asked to accept parts of you that are not to his perfect liking. This does not mean dysfunctional traits, but the peculiar little things that make us individuals. Some are cute, some are misunderstood, and some even annoying in an acceptable way. In other words, as long as this is who he really is, you must be prepared to accept him at face value.

There are also learned habits and behaviors which cause pause and need to be further explored and experienced. For example, inability to engage in meaningful discussion to resolve issues, is something to look into. This may be linked to childhood issues, ignorance, or merely lack of practice. In any event, this is not acceptable behavior, or you will find this person building walls of isolation and resentment rather than communicating. Someone who is rude, discourteous, and lacking manners has to be inquired upon as to why this is so. Impatience is another practice which should cause us to pause and have a deeper look, because it has all sorts of implications. If we are to believe that *patience* is another word for *love*, then there is definitely a problem that requires resolution. When behaviors of any curious nature surface, this becomes the work of the day, and must be addressed. Go toward the early signs of behaviors that send up red flags, and learn how to manage, address, and eliminate them as you do. Discussion, cooperation and observation will bring this to the surface. Any resistance to a healthy pursuit or inquiry is a red flag. Healthy dialogue is mandatory to growth, and will promote understanding and healing. No elephants in the room for you! You must not feel afraid to speak or inquire about anything that bothers you or needs addressing. Elephants must be indentified, addressed, then released back into the wild. Also be aware of people who are stuck. They are argumentative, closed-minded, and believe only one way. Their energy is weak from having to maintenance their limbo, and their world remains small. Being captive to other forces and unhappy with themselves, they seek above all else, company for their own misery. None of that for you.

Girl Pearl: *The heart is wiser than the intellect.*

Dating is a Process

The man you are considering to date, marry, or be friends with, should be introduced to your family, neighbors and friends, and be exposed to as many different situations as possible. Your role will be to see how he handles himself in these situations, how he interacts with different people, and what actions he takes as various circumstances present themselves. Listen, watch, and ask questions. Include in this *getting to know you* stage, exposure to pets, nature, and children.

What you are looking for is what comes out of this person in different scenarios and situations. This will give you a glimpse of what is in his heart. Fine garments, a fancy car, a good job, manners, wealth, good looks and all the rest are fine and dandy, but they do not reveal the heart of a person. In fact, they confuse you and distort your journey. Be aware that he will practice good manners, etiquette and courtesies, so watch for contradictions in his character, nature or speech. This is by no means for purposes of judgment. It is merely being aware and attuned, to assist you in identifying the red flags which are always present, but which we often ignore. As you continue this process of observation, the most critical part, and the part most often ignored is this: **never doubt what you see.** This is where we all fail. After everything goes south, the true character is revealed and we finally see it years down the line, 95 percent of us can say: *I saw those early warning signs, but I ignored them.* Use time and circumstances to reveal the whole story. It is very difficult, even for the best of the best deceivers, to hide themselves for as much as a year. So rather than spend one year to *out* someone, expose them to as many scenarios as you can, and trust in what you see and hear. It is worth saying again another way: **never doubt what you see and hear**. Don't dismiss or excuse anything, do not make judgments, but *do* make *notes to self.* Make the necessary allowances for human flaws, letting time be your best friend.

A woman who dated a man for months, was shocked one day to see him get very angry in a restaurant when a waiter disappeared for a length of time. This man become so upset that when the waiter did show up, he berated him in public for being negligent, and the woman was horrified at the lack of common sense and composure in his behavior. She had no trouble imagining that one day down the line she could be that berated waiter. She recognized that this man had some work to do, and that if she was to continue seeing him, it would be with the understanding that he get counseling. If you do not take action when these behaviors are revealed to you, what you are seeing is your own future, and it won't be pretty. Resist...resist...resist the temptation to talk yourself into believing the behavior will correct itself. Making this assumption is a flaw in *you*, and is discussed liberally throughout the book.

There are many good, innocent, fun, yet revealing ways to discover what is in a person. Have fun with this! Consider a trip to Disneyland, for instance. Taking the rides, snacking, waiting in line, interacting with the crowds and watching the parades, are conducive environments for a person's more revealing side to come out and play, because he is relaxed, at ease and off guard. What does he do if a child turns and blindly runs into him? Is he patient and courteous while waiting in line or is he self-serving and impatient? Is he drawing negative attention to himself in any way? In large crowds, is he critical of others? Does he ogle at other women? Does he minimize his relationship with you in the company of an attractive woman? While driving, how does he handle another driver cutting him off? Does he get angry? Is he retaliatory? Does he curse or make obscene gestures? Playing games of any kind can also bring out revealing aspects of human nature. Does he play fairly, or does he cheat to win? Does he get angry when he loses? How does he behave in sports games and competitions? Is he excessively competitive? Quick to anger? Hostile toward other players? All these activities…going out to different eating places, movies, bowling, day traveling, road trips, group dating, skating, sports events, shooting pool, and having coffee or tea, are opportunities for both fun and observation. Enjoy yourself, be light-hearted and fun, and be ever vigilant in seeing and hearing, and not doubting what you see and hear. As a side note, this is also an opportunity for you to observe yourself and what comes out of you in these situations. Not only are you looking for attractive virtues and attributes in a man…he is looking for the same in you. You are in the process of becoming a real woman….use this time to your advantage as well, and it will keep you from the temptation of judging another.

Girl Pearl: *When one finds a worthy wife, her value is far beyond pearls. Her husband, entrusting his heart to her, has an unfailing prize.*

174

Make Friends with Time

While you are dating and waiting, you will discover things about the person that bother, amuse, confuse, and mislead you. No worries, however, as time and honest discussion will help you deal with all this. There are some things about him you will be able to easily understand and accept. For example, if you like to cook and your intended date is a picky eater, ask yourself if this is something you can live with. If so, go into it that way and accept it. However, if you discover during your outings that your intended does not enjoy meeting people, but does it as an accommodation to you, who happens to love meeting people, then you may have an issue that makes you incompatible. If you learn to stay in the moment and observe, the system, along with time, works wonderfully. As situations are presented for your examination, evaluate them inwardly and you will know what to do with them at the time. Whatever behavior you see or hear, you'll know it going in, and either accept it or do not proceed past this point with dating unless it is merely for fun, friendship or amusement purposes.

When it comes to dating, boys, men or males like to get right to the point, and therefore, consider the dating game a chore. They treat it as such because it's an unknown world to them. They prefer, and may treat it as a hunt, which, of course, culminates into a kill. This they understand. They like to start something then finish it. Dating remains unexplored territory for most guys. They may not want to date someone who isn't going to give in to them, now or in the future. They want closure on anything they begin, thus dating may tend to be illusive for some. From your perspective, what's the hurry anyway? Remember, if you are needy, then you're missing something that has to be dealt with between you and yourself. Outside forces cannot cure inside aches and pains. If you are lacking in this area, the highest form of helping yourself is letting your heart plot the course and not your mind and emotions.

Girl Pearl: *There are no impossible dreams.*

175

Make Him Angry!

The main point of my entire book is for you to find out who someone really is. Who you are, and who he is. If he doesn't come out willingly, as described in various chapters, then there's a sure-fired way to find out what's inside him, and what makes this guy tick. Make him upset or angry. Yes, you read it right. To see what comes out of this man, and what is really inside him, anger is the perfect way to get an unrehearsed and spontaneous response. You see, with anger, a person has no time to pretend or plan a response, so what is in someone comes out right then and there. Now, to some of you, this may be a shocking statement. Why should it be? Stories abound of mean, angry men, whose cruelty was only discovered after the fact. What is wrong with knowing about it before hand? How a person handles conflict, dispute, challenge, shock, and temptation is very important to know. This concept is not new, either. Oftentimes, people who apply for high-level or high-maintenance positions, where the job requirements include substantial "people contact" or multi-million dollar investments in various fields, are led down this road and tested by their interviewers and company management.

Now, I'm not suggesting you walk up to the candidate and slap him. However, look for the opportunity for his anger to come out, then watch, listen and learn. Be quick to explore what happened, how he handled his response, and his willingness to converse about it. Things will come up for both of you, that if you are willing to do the work now, will serve you very well later. No weapon can come against you when you seek to improve, correct, and live a decent and right life. Make mistakes, but handle them, then get right back into the mix. Remember, here is a person that you are dating, or wanting to know better. Just be aware of what is going on, and know that two people who really care about each other, can take on difficulties together and get things done if they go about it the right way.

Girl Pearl: *Wherever you go, whatever you do, or whatever you choose to say, go, do and say with all your heart.*

No Sex...It Complicates Things

The sex act was never intended for the mockery and entertainment it has become. Mankind took it to that extreme. Use your own common sense to explore this. The Creator of all life and goodness created a planet, and from the dust of it made a human being, and breathed into him the breath of life. The first man was born, a magnificent creature unlike any other. Then, man began to discover that the place which had been prepared for him, this place called earth, was teeming with life. He began to understand that he was an eternal being, living in a place where there was plenty to explore and discover. After a quick nap one day, he awakened to something he could never have imagined, but would love, want and cherish all his life. What words could he have formed in that moment of over-whelming joy? After having given names to all the animals, having seen them all in pairs, he awakened to behold a companion of his own like-kind, a magnificent mate fitted perfectly to him. Eve truly was God's gift to man: an expression of love to Adam by the Source of *all* love. She was a companion to share the life experience with, to adventure and explore with, a helpmate, friend, and simply put, she was *company to man.* Now there were *two* coming forth together to delight the whole world and everything in it, including even the animals. These two were God's expression of divine artistry, and the crowning glory of creation.

It was only after their well-documented boo-boo, that sex was promoted to the front lines and became too important for its own good. Prior to that, for this first couple, being together and sharing with each other unconditionally, was the joy. Wanting to see each other was the reward. In this day, sex has worked its way up to become a substitute for the inner life, when it was designed to be a compliment to it. It has developed a life of its own. Man has perverted it, and in turn, it makes a mockery of man, sparing no one. We have taken what should be a modest, discreet and reserved subject, and turned it into mainstream debauchery. It is the *individual* who must bring respect to this subject matter, and you are that individual!

177

As you journey through life, you become aware that all things are possible. If you can think it, it can be done. In America, this dynamic is even more at play because of our freedoms. With all our choices come heavy responsibility, which simply and literally means: the ability to respond. Moderation, abstinence and "less is more" dynamics will provide you with a quality ticket to explore and experience all life has to offer. Now, let's apply this to sex.....

Should one wish to ignore the *no sex* rule, one can surely do it, but it will be at a high cost, and requires high maintenance. You will be distracted from the real and the genuine, and will not be practicing your higher calling. As long as you know what you're getting into, all I can ask is that you maintain that awareness and do not lose yourself in this. It is a poor substitute for your wants and needs. It's like a drug to those who practice sex before, or outside marriage. It becomes a bad habit (when practiced for the wrong reasons) which is hard to be rid of, even if you are conscious of it.

The older and wiser woman, the one with experience in life, has quite a bit to say about men and sex. You see, there is nothing new on this subject, except when you are considering getting into it. Once you've been sexually active for awhile, you will know everything, but at what price? Did you use it or did it use you? If you are able to trust and open up to any wise woman, she will tell you what she has learned (if she can get past the embarrassment). Lend her your ear and gather data. Women like to help other women, and will do so freely. The sisterhood always works! The sex act has its place, and it should be a place of honor, but what do you do with the rest of the day? What a potent question to ask and have answered. How about this question: Can a man enjoy a woman without having to *have* her? Males fail to look into this, and women don't hold them accountable to it. Once a man stops or slows down his appetite long enough to see another side of a woman's beauty, his perspective begins to change. It is up to the woman to teach him correctly, and then a different kind of love goes to work.

A common misconception between men and women, is that a woman may assume sex implies a commitment, where the man may not see it that way. Already, this is starting out on the wrong foot, and eventually will end up taking you somewhere other than where you wanted to be. How you begin something often determines where you will end up. So, here you see where the woman literally gives all she has, expecting he will give all he has in return. The male sees it differently. He doesn't consider sex to be an unspoken commitment, because he already managed to get all he wanted without much effort, and now, maintaining what he has is the only effort he needs to make. Consequently, there will be no real, long-term, intimate connection. He also knows he will have at it again and again. Men tend to think in pretty clear and simple dynamics. So now, we have an elephant in the room. It becomes much more difficult to objectively see each other's character traits when sex is at work. From there, some couples then slide into engagement and marriage only to discover they have missed seeing major aspects of each other because their perspectives were clouded by premature and irresponsible intimacy. If you skip steps, you skip out on the vital parts of who you are, what you are feeling, and what you should be looking for in him. These critical areas will get neither addressed nor fed, and will create a void that will not go away.

Realize there are emotional consequences for getting involved in a sexual relationship, and if you are trying to find someone who loves you for who you are, and visa versa, you must leave sex out of it. There is so much to be explored and appreciated during the dating process, and plenty of time for the exploration of sex under the right conditions. After marriage, sex can help you explore intimate issues in a responsible way. It is a timely and reward-able gift, and when activated correctly, can satisfy and go the long distance with honor and nobility. God will even join you and activate his promises. Leave this alone for now. For dating it is not needed, and for courting it is not profitable.

Those who have been damaged by exposing too much of themselves incorrectly and before their time, have learned to enclose their hearts with a protective shield resembling stone. While this barrier does protect its bearer very well, it creates a prison at the same time. Consequently you cannot get out nor can anyone else get in. It is never too late to undo this dynamic. Usually, resentment for an injustice that has taken place will be found lurking in the background. So, your first step will be to realize this and then to repent of the resentment. To do so, you may have to revisit the circumstances via counseling or meditation, although neither is required. Once the resentment is lifted, you propel yourself into *the moment* and out of the past where you were bound. Staying behind a wall, from where you cannot come out and others cannot come in, profits no one. Why not avoid all that and seek what is true, right, fair, just, and meaningful for the right reasons? In other words, start out on the right foot. In that journey, you will find all your needs met and your true purpose awaiting you. No unnecessary baggage will be formed, no regrets, and your heart will be light and airy like that of a child. You will then have peace not of this world, life abundant, and joy everlasting as your reward.

It must be said, that it may be extremely difficult to resist the temptation of sex while it seems so gratifying to your emotional needs at the time. So I urge you to remember this: that which is so strong in the moment often becomes loathsome in memory, whether its name be anger, sex, revenge, gossip, ridicule or mockery. Take heed not to follow your burning wish lest you later be needing the sorrow of repentance.

Girl Pearl: On using seduction, innocence, naïveté, availability, and attraction on a male: You can employ any of these methods to catch a guy, but you are now bound to him through this conduct and must sustain it to keep him. When you tire of this and want to start being yourself, it won't be good enough.

Sexual Pressure, Bluffs & Ultimatums

Ladies, if you've been seriously dating someone for a period of time, the question of becoming physically engaged will most likely come up at some point. Perhaps it already has, and you've taken a stand on celibacy, and have made it clear to him. At the same time you are beginning to trust him, you may also be experiencing feelings of love for him. It is at this time you become extremely vulnerable, and if he is a dishonorable man, he will use this to his advantage in a deceptive way. To all appearances, this man has been patient with you, and has demonstrated care and accountability to you. He brings up the subject of lovemaking, under the seemingly sincere declaration of his "love." You believe he loves you, so you continue to take your stand of celibacy, just as you have before, fully trusting his love. But he has also become sure of your deep feelings for him. He is aware you don't want to lose him, so he inquires again. Still, you stand. Now, right out of his bag of tricks and deceptions, he pulls the big bluff. He has set the stage, has waited patiently for this day, has perfected his timing so there is little risk to himself, and he proceeds with what should be for you a *huge* red flag, which may come in different words than these, but their import will be the same, when he says: "well, okay then, maybe we shouldn't see each other for awhile." Did you hear that? What he just did was to give you a subtle indication that the relationship is over. Actually, it was not so subtle, he just didn't use the words *"it's over."*

What you do in this moment of truth will change the course of the rest of your life. He has just shown another side of himself, and *you saw it*, but you are also vulnerable. You may think if you don't engage physically with him that the relationship will be over, and you've just begun to have hopes of its progression. Here is where it can become confusing, especially for a younger woman. You do not want to lose him. You have become comfortable and are advancing toward committing more of yourself, but that does not include sharing your body. You want this person, but do not want to give in to his demands. You have been set up, girls, because you should not be experiencing this, and you wouldn't be with an honest or

181

decent man. So now, his problem has become your problem, and your mind and emotions are reeling. Does he love me or just want my body? Is sex required if the relationship is to continue? If I don't do it, will he discontinue seeing me? Will he do it with someone else? If I do it, will I eventually lose him or his respect? You have opened the proverbial can of worms.

The very principles of your character are being tested. You KNOW in your heart what just happened. He gave you an ultimatum. He didn't call it that, no, he's much too selfish to call it an ultimatum. A life lived without morals is less of a life. Now, on the inside of you is a conflict, and you have two roads set before you. One road is long, hard, wide, well traveled and uncertain, even if you should one day marry him. The other road is narrow and less traveled, but is the road of truth, virtue, justice and right, whose path is exceedingly certain, although you cannot see that now. The choice has been presented, and your future, your fate and even all of heaven awaits your answer. Girls of all ages: stand. Take your stand in this moment, and it may turn out to be the most righteous stand you will ever take. If you risk letting him go for righteousness sake, know this one thing: that in the very moment you take your stand for what you believe, somewhere in the invisible world, your true and intended love will begin making his way toward you. This is your defining moment. It is your moment of truth. The direction of your life hangs in the balances, awaiting your answer. Choose wisely and you'll never be sorry. If you are not able to choose, pause and let time speak to your heart and his.

In the alternative, choosing the road this man has set you up for, will summon another set of dynamics down upon you and your future. Dark and unrewarding energy is at work, perhaps satisfying in the moment, but never satisfying in itself. You will always be back for more, because now you have begun an addiction to something that is wrong, and that wrong has entered into you, lives in you, and needs to be fed. The world, your own unchecked animal behavior, and dark forces teach another discipline, one that *owns you* as you practice it. You start out thinking you have control of it, and indeed this may be true in the early conception of any animal-like behavior.

However, as you continue with it, at some point a subtle shift takes place of which you are entirely unaware. The shift is actually a transfer...the transfer of power from you to "it." The "behavior" you once thought to control, now has control of you. It possesses you, and you have become its slave without your knowledge, but with your full permission, for which you will one day find yourself responsible. A man who will take you without honor and before your time, is using you, and if you do not know it now, you will discover it later. If you allow him to do it, you have given up your honor also. Two dishonorable people do not an honorable person make. In due time, you will have an overwhelming temptation to resent the man. He will hate you for hating him, and it can all be tracked down to this ill-timed intimacy which came about in a dishonorable way. The woman who allows herself to be used, may never tire of the attention that comes with being used, but inside will have the company of a giant void where she and God never connected, and where her inner parts were not allowed to grow, prosper, and be shared correctly. Remember the rule: short-term pain brings long-term pleasure. The pain of the hard work necessary to achieve something of value is short-term, yet has long-term payoffs. Backwards living is short-term pleasure for long-term pain. Talk with your fellow sisters who have traveled this way. All of them regret having given in to this dynamic. They will tell you that things didn't go well for them short or long-term. Should you choose this road, you will be *used,* and worse, you will have allowed yourself to be used. It is only later, down the road, that you will begin to realize you had been seduced.

Dear ladies...if you have not learned it yet, please consider this: never use sex to hold onto a man. If he requires it for the relationship to continue, let him walk...he does not love you, and that is the pure and simple truth. Intimacy comes with time, trust and vulnerability. Fallen human nature dictates that when people get all they want of anything, they quickly devalue it. Sex is a portion of the intimate process that should be handled with extreme and tender care... starting with privacy, right timing and pure motives. As God himself makes no claims upon us by way of demand, only desiring that we come to him willingly, so must it be in the man/woman relationship if it is to prosper and be fulfilling to both persons. The subject of a life companion is one to be elevated to the stars and beyond, because it deserves just that kind of attention.

An important point to consider is that sometime in your life (and for some of you right now), you will be going through menopause. It begins at different times for women, somewhere between ages 35 through 55. During that time of life, women often experience a strong desire to right all their wrongs, including being taken before their time, and taken the wrong way. They realize they were dishonored, abused, used, and disrespected, and they see the part they played in it. Menopause empowers them through hormones, clarity of mind, wrongs surfacing within them, and *right* being their new standard when it comes to their well-being. Woe to the man who doesn't come clean at this time or before. An apology is in order from the many who have taken a woman before her time, in the wrong way, or used her in any way. She, in turn, will never allow anyone to do it again. Avoid all this, now that you know about it. If the man loves you, he wants your well-being above all, and the reward for his right motives is your true love for him. If a man does his part correctly, he gains an additional heart (yours). Now you have a man with two hearts, and two hearts can accomplish and contribute quite a bit of loving to this world.

Whatever time and attention a man puts into a woman determines what he will get from her in return. As he gives her security, love, attentiveness, understanding, compassion, tenderness, friendship, counsel and loyalty, when he holds, comforts, supports and accepts her, and loves her for no other reason than that she's herself, then he is prized by her in return. When a woman gets her needs met, everyone gains for the right reasons, and she blooms like a flower. When a flower blossoms, beauty is upon you and defined without words. Yet even the pretty flower requires pollen from the bee, and not just any old passing pollen fancy either. The bee must invest for the flower to bloom and prosper.

Girl Pearl: The true test of love is what one is willing to do for others.

184

Women: Toys or Treasures?

The answer to this is entirely up to you. You set the standard and decide in what direction it will progress. If you approach a relationship promising wonderful sexual escapades and undying worship and service, then be prepared to keep that up, because you are training him in to accept it. When you tire or withdraw, or simply want more meaning and depth beyond that, don't be surprised if he rebels. You were not put here to become the exclusive physical play toy for a man. Toys get abused, abandoned, broken then discarded.

Your true purpose runs as deep as you do. Considering your complexity, the depth and faithfulness of your heart, your nurturing, protective nature and your feminine perspective on life, imagine the depth of your needs as well. The intimate coming together of a man and a woman is not a frivolous act, but one that has deep, divine purpose for both. A friend, companion, devotee, confidant, helpmate, steady date, business

185

partner, and much more awaits some lucky fellow. There is so much to offer, yet somehow your body enters into the primary role of the relationship, and the rest of you goes neglected. This will happen only if you allow it. I have a hard time believing that the moment Adam saw Eve, they made love day and night. Sounds pretty needy to me, and quite cheap and common. I have been lucky enough to interact with some extraordinary women in my life. I was glad to have known them, and prospered because of it. When everyone comes to sincerely appreciate another person's position on this planet, and their reason for being here, life takes on new meaning, and a fascinating one at that.

Girl Pearl: Have you ever passed a display of beautiful diamonds or pearls and ooohed and aahhhed? Well, you are that beauty you so much admire.

Sex is Not Love....no! no! no!

There is a common misconception among women, especially young women, that sex is an indication of love. Sex and love are not the same, and they'll never be the same. Most women don't understand this, because to the feminine nature, with rare exceptions, sex is an outward demonstration of love. For a feminine woman, having sex without love is nearly impossible. Therefore, because *she* feels this way, she naturally assumes this is the case with the man. This is not so with the ani-male. Lust is as far away from love as the east is from the west. A good man should be able to enjoy a woman's company without "having" her. A woman can sense when this is the case. However, women want to be held, loved and cherished, and want to spend time with their special person. In the pursuit of that dream, they may make wrong choices. Righteousness, or the pursuit of the right way should take precedence in all you do. St. Augustus said "love first and then do what you will." We

186

do well to listen to him, for love must be first before all. In regard to sex, if the man is not willing to abstain, then you are in for rough seas ahead, and if you give in, the "love" you accepted in the short-term will soon expire. Where will you be then? You young girls should seek the advice of the older women who have traveled this road. They would have much to say to a good listener. Sex and love are two different dynamics. Mixing the two is a sure cocktail designed to rob you of the true drink of life.

Promiscuous behavior is self-defining. Keep in mind that if it walks, talks and acts like a duck, the quacking shouldn't shock you. Being loose with moral behavior and beliefs leads to the dumbing down of a human being, and to becoming less of a person and more of a body part. Your body should not define who you are. It is the "you" inside your body that is precious, valuable, worthy of respect and to be treated well, first by you, and then by others. Think how all this started. God wanted you, and you wanted to be wanted. It was mutual, unconditional, and love-driven. It wasn't until later when things went south, that substitutes and additives for happiness and love (or what we think is happiness and love) were applied. Whatever happened after that is deplorable and unacceptable, but in effect all over this planet. Sex has become more important than it should be. For some people, the pleasure derived from it has become a substitute for life. Women are now looked upon in a way where they can be used for that purpose first and everything else second. That was not the intent of the Creator. Any man that plays a part in the dysfunction of sex with a woman is no longer a man but an animal or ani-male. This is the current state of affairs, yet we think of it as normal and acceptable. Wake up! We are all being selfishly fooled while indulging for the wrong reasons.

Girl Pearl: A man should offer his wife a new kind of security. It is the security of knowing that he is loyal for love's sake, good for goodness' sake, and not just a bee after the honey.

Teen Sex

Where does one begin on a subject like this? What does a teenager know about anything besides being a teenager who doesn't know about anything? Well, except texting, email, and cell phones. Many of us didn't seize the opportunities presented by high school. I can remember quite a few good girls who had unhealthy home environments getting into trouble early on. It is not easy growing up, having more questions than answers, and in many circumstances, not knowing who to ask. They may not even know what or how to ask, let alone what to make of the answers. This is precisely why teenagers need to be *told*, and why it is profitable for parents to take the initiative and *talk*. Teens need to be looked after, watched, nurtured, and protected until their common sense kicks in. It's that age in life where they have begun to see a few important truths, and now think they know everything. Truths will come to them slowly, and sometimes with hard lessons, to be handled accordingly and with proper supervision. Unfortunately, many parents are not up to the task, and some teens don't offer a lot of cooperation. The pressures that come upon the heads of the households from having a home, responsibilities, expenses, and difficult choices, abound, and affect everyone. Add to all this the fact that parents never parented before, neither did their parents or their parents' parents, and so on. Consequently, the majority of parents learn as they go and do the best they can. So, how does one get answers to a subject like this? By discussing it.

There are many reasons teens give for having sex:

- everyone is doing it (not acceptable)
- curiosity
- hormones which remain misunderstood drive erratic behavior
- misplaced love (i.e. sex is substituted for genuine, deep caring and sharing)
- escape from a not so good life
- boredom
- rebellion
- temptation

188

- opportunity
- rape or molestation

To be introduced to such a mature subject at a tender age is traumatic. The human machine is capable of extraordinary accomplishments and has been given magnificent survival techniques, but subjecting it to the unnecessary and premature stress and trauma of sex, with all its dangers and emotional upheavals, will have long-term effects. Everything has its timing. There is no better example of this than the four seasons. Each season sets up the other and goes round and round. If one season doesn't act predictably, it throws off the other seasons and affects that yearly cycle. This is what happens to human beings, on a multitude of subjects, and for many reasons. A child is born, and with joy, has been invited to the wonder of life. The parents rejoice, are full of hope and expectation, and have every confidence that the seasons of life will flow as they ought to. Indeed they are meant to and they should, but they do not. They're not predictable, and with their changes come storms of dissention, the heat of anger, the winds of temptation, the chill of hate and the floods of sorrow. There are interruptions, delays, traumas, hardships, abuses and sometimes divorce and death. All this has children growing up before their time. Keep to your childhood season, flow with it and enjoy it for as long as possible, for it is a brief season already, and soon enough you will come into adulthood with all its challenges. Arrive there with as pure and innocent a heart as you can maintain, with what has been presented to you.

Sex before your time is something that can injure you unexpectedly, without you realizing the damage that has been done until years down the line when it all begins to catch up with you. There is the tremendous emotional aspect of it, especially for very young women, which can corrupt the child in you and cause the adult to come forth injured and unhealthy, all because it was compelled to come out before its season had arrived. The boys your age are not ready for commitment and marriage, anymore than you are, and yet your emotions as a teen will tell you he's the only one in the world for you. You do not yet realize that he will come and go, and the world will go on, and yes, even *your* world will go on. As a teenager, if the guy is even just a few years older than you, there's more reason to be extremely guarded, because there's a great probability he is there to use you and break your heart and you don't even know it.

There is the stressful consequence of a potential unplanned pregnancy, and having to confront and learn about this subject the hard way. This breaks the hearts of everyone involved, including yours. Some teens want to "play dolls" again, and get pregnant to have someone to love, or more importantly to them, someone to be loved *by*. Of course, the responsibilities involved when this occurs before its time, become overwhelming. Remember, having children is a minimum 20-year commitment. Do you really want to start this heavy responsibility so early in your own young life? Girls that have had to make these decisions, regretted having to deal with this at an early age, having missed what they didn't realize was still part of their childhood. The guilt they endured from wanting to do other things while having to care for a child, proved to be very challenging.

Growing up is an interesting phenomenon for all of us. Some of us have the most pleasant memories and opportunities, and others have endured pure hell with everything in between. My counsel to anyone going through hard times, confusion, doubt, growth factors, dysfunction, and *need,* should *not* add the dynamics of sex to their problems. For anyone that has already done the deed, *stop doing it right now!* Be sorry for getting ahead of yourself, and you can create a fresh start. (See Repentance chapter.) You will know when the time has come to visit or revisit this subject, and then you will be ready for it emotionally, psychologically, mentally, physically and spiritually. Best to you on this.

Girl Pearl: *The highest love a man can attain is to merge his soul with God. Loving you after this will be heaven on earth.*

Masturbation...You Won't Go Blind

What in the world is this subject doing in a dating book? That is a fair question. Hormones in some people can be strong and interfere with their thinking. How you handle this situation is very important. The sexual tension, which is a combination of your whole body lining up with God's commandment to multiply, creates a stress of the sort that builds up in some people making them potentially more vulnerable. The way I see it, you have four choices:

(1) Live with the awareness that your body is crying out, and answer the cry by disciplining yourself. Know that the body's cry is there waiting, and in time it will either pass or subside naturally. It is like a hunger pang that will subside when not immediately answered. Eventually, the call to arms weakens, and your desire is contained. Stand this ground as long as you can. Over time, it will submit to you, and you will learn to handle it when it does. **NOTE:** You do not want to trigger this phenomenon before its time. Premature awakening may put you under its influence before your time has come to handle it, and may interfere with your true destiny. You do not want to become a slave to this, like overeating or out-of-control emotions.

(2) Manually stimulate yourself. If it becomes unbearable or you obsess with it, then relieve yourself. Do not make a drama or soap opera out of it. Stay out of your mind as much as possible. This is preferable to seeking men out and becoming promiscuous as you explore. The ways both men and women refer to a loose woman is not nice.

(3) Have protected sex. As far as I see it, this will put you on a course that is available, but not the true one. Think this through and ask yourself, *what is the hurry?* It cannot be undone. Also, you trigger dangerous dynamics by doing this. Known and visible laws govern us in everything we do. The Ten Commandments (and more) were created to help the race of Jews survive when other tribes were dying out from lack of law or discipline

to govern themselves. If you venture outside these laws designed to help you, you enter into a realm of *other* laws that work also, but not to your advantage. You should never let your impulses or anything else control you.

(4) Wait until all the ducks line up correctly and quack the love song (my hope for you). Be advised that you don't want to use the masturbation act as a reason not to risk, or to put off, intimacy when the right time does present itself. You must learn to save yourself even from yourself.

Girl Pearl: Every diamond or pearl that came into the world has a unique story to tell. Girls, what is your story going to be?

Dating Guys with Children

This is an interesting subject, especially if you are facing it. Dating and getting to know each other, is already a full-time endeavor. Adding anything to that is nothing short of a lot to take on. Sure, if he is a good catch, then you will gain by having the two of you take on all of life's problems together. In theory, it sounds great. However, children who are involved in single parent scenarios, don't always do well with a parent's dating scenes. The majority of children are angry, confused, bitter, and downright against replacing mom or dad. At some point, you'll be taking this on too.

There are various reasons someone may consider dating and accepting guys with children. Perhaps you couldn't have children of your own; or you do have your own children, you're domestically inclined, and like family environments; or it comes with accepting Mr. Right. Your thinking may be: *the more the merrier.* Regardless of the reason, go into this with both eyes open, and realize that it may be tough on everyone going in. I don't expect you to cure all the problems that come up, but you must be able to handle them when they do. Knowing this, proceed with patience, teamwork, and commitment. However, my final point is one I hope you heed, and it is this: If you are not able or willing to open your heart to love his children, then you have no business dating or marrying him. If you have feelings of jealousy over them, or you are able to see that loving them will be difficult or impossible for you, then for the children's sake, for his sake, for your sake and for God's sake don't get involved.

Girl Pearl*: The only time things become difficult for a woman is when she has to deal with a man.*

Dating & Single Moms

Alright ladies…we need to assess your situation if, for whatever reason, you are a mom and now single. Your priorities must be straight. First priority is the child or children. They have to be protected and loved during this difficult transition period. They come first and I am counting on you during this time to stay composed and focused. Your needs must come second or go on hold altogether. Do this willingly and not begrudgingly. If your children are very young, they will not yet experience the shaking up or the breaking up of the family or circumstances. This allows you some time to get settled into a new lifestyle. If they are old enough to know that the father is missing, they become the squeaky wheel, and need lots of oil for their needs to be addressed. You must offer physical, emotional, and psychological assurances that all is well. They are sensing the changes, but are not able to voice them. They may, however, act those changes out in their behaviors, which will require your attention and correction. This is a good time to maintain contact with family and friends for support.

Developing and keeping to daily routines as much as possible, will give them a sense of stability. They are able to sense your motives for whatever you do. As you maintain a calm and relaxed demeanor, they will gain a sense of security that all is well, and follow your example. Be aware that too much emotion in your voice or in your actions may betray you, and a lack of patience in your conduct and attitude will injure and confuse them. So, be aware, be calm and be the parent you need to be, and in time you will get through this just fine. It will end when it ends, and you'll need to practice this discipline that you've been thrust into, correctly and effectively.

Now, women with children may (or may not) have a tougher go at dating than those without children. But that won't be your issue unless you let it be. To find someone who is willing to love you and your children may require additional time and attention. During this time, you may even meet someone who is in a similar situation, and can explore the practicality of dating and waiting, then eventually joining forces for the betterment of all. Finding someone in this world is not difficult in any way. Finding the *right* one and making it work can be, if we do not pay the proper mind to it. Never give up on wanting to share yourself with someone, but not at any price or at the cost of your identity, welfare, or your children's welfare. In any event, if you take the time to right any wrongs and give care to yourself, love will have a way of finding you. So, we are back to the basics of making ourselves attractive from the inside, spending quality time and attention on ourselves, and then going outside to explore the possibilities to be found within us and around us. It is very important not to transmit neediness, low self-esteem, unworthiness or *woe is me...I will do anything to be loved* vibes. I have seen women who have just given up and will settle for the first warm body that comes around. Talk to some of your more experienced sisters out there. Being married to, or living with, someone you don't love, eventually turns you into a bitter beast. It is not worth it, and others who have gone before you will tell you this. Many of you may have seen this in your own parents growing up.

Now, with all that out of the way, a question arises. Should you tell prospective dates that you have children? If they are small children, I would definitely do so. Some guys will not want to deal with the family aspect at this time. Fine, we can weed them out of the mix. You may find yourself meeting other single parents where you will now have the children issue in common. You may explore that at your leisure, becoming aware of the pros and cons of what the future may hold. Be aware that love may not be the governing factor for some, as you move forward. Love is a very rewarding exercise for the human being. Sometimes it can take a back seat to your personal reality. You may be wanting to explore the economic necessity or formal arrangements and benefits of leaving your heart in second place. That is entirely up to you and your circumstances. Just be aware of it going in.

Girl Pearl: Attracting a man solely by using your body, may meet your body's needs, but not those of your heart.

Prior to Pregnancy...Hit the Pause Button

A large segment of the population has had unwanted or unexpected children as a result of a liaison between two people looking for instant gratification and acting irresponsibly. I also know of women who are not maternal and males who are not paternal. These types do not want to be parents, and the children suffer because of it. You may have been one of these children, or you may be dating someone who is. Others have traveled this way before you, and you will do well to learn from them. Do not give in to the passions and hormones of the moment, or to weaknesses and promises that will lead to getting pregnant for the wrong reasons.

I must also address the subject of a woman considering hooking a guy by getting pregnant. This is not an original thought. It has been used over the centuries, and many have suffered from this type of manipulation. Imagine the dark thoughts and underhanded planning that go into implementing this. Do not make friends with deception, for it will prove itself a treacherous friend in the end. If this is what you think it takes to get him, then consider asking and answering the following questions in the secrecy of your own heart and conscience: Why would you want to be with a man who doesn't love you enough to marry you in the first place? Is this what it takes for you to get him? Do you feel that what you are offering is not good enough and therefore this is your only way of holding onto him? Do you think having his baby will cause him to love you if he doesn't already? Do you consider the possibility that doing this may cause him to resent you? Stop, look inward, and begin the process of self-examination and introspection. If he loves you already, nearly anything you do will cause him to love you more; if he doesn't love you, *nothing* you do will awaken what is not there, whether it be affection, kindness, wittiness, adoration, devotion, or having his baby. If you are considering this out of desperation, then you are not ready…you have work to do.

For those of you considering having a baby in order to have someone (the baby) to love, and love you back, I have this to say: Your desire is sound, but your motives are not. Also, please ask yourself, how can you love someone else correctly, while you're in desperate need of that much love yourself? At some point, your needs will not get met, and the baby, who needs your one hundred percent commitment, will suffer being denied it. Girls, there is a way to go about all this that doesn't create new problems as you go. For those of you who have already had a child, you must finish what you have started. Prioritize and balance your life, work with your circumstances, always doing the right thing when it presents itself. You may suffer from having made some poor decisions, but in time it will work itself out if you do the work required to bring about the changes.

People in jail, and even some in hospitals, wish they could relive those several moments before their poor choices became a reality. Add to this list pregnancy. Being pregnant before your time will earn you a Diploma from the School of Hard Knocks. You do not want this diploma, and you do not want to attend this school. Never give control of yourself over to anyone or anything. Be anxious for nothing, and do not let your emotions run your life. Let this statement trickle down

196

from your brain, onto your tongue, and melt in your mouth. Savor it. It is grievous to think of all the children born unwanted, the products of lust. Many of you have experienced this first hand. *Pause* and *time-out* should be your very best friends. Impulses, temptations, hormones, bad advice, and poor choices are all standing in line, waiting to have their way with you. They do not have your interest at heart, nor do they respect you. Their agenda is to see you fail and to travel into a life of misery, regret and deprivation. Waking up after the fact is doable, but for those who have not yet been ensnared, pause and pause often. Ask questions of everyone, but continue to make up your own mind. Learn to recognize and interact with your own conscience and common sense. It will never fail or abandon you...ever.

Pausing also works well when deciding whether to go out with someone, where to go if you do, and what to do when you get there. When in doubt, invoke the pause clause and listen to your conscience. If others have difficulty with it, let them deal with their own pausing issues, because yours are non-negotiable. In fact, if someone is attempting to force you against your pause, that is a sure-fired red flag warning to pause even further. In your own life, you may already have occasions where, in hindsight you wished you had taken a pause, and other times, how glad you were that you did! You see, it works if you use it.

Girl Pearl: To regard another's health, wealth, welfare, happiness, feelings, needs, and aspirations equal to or above your own, is to love them.

Date Rape Happens

Many years ago, for a period of two years, I volunteered as a rape counselor for a small California city. Ladies, the stories I heard were enough to last a lifetime. Even the

197

therapists had to counsel each other due to the high emotional, mental, and psychological stress brought on by forced sexual behavior perpetrated upon women. For some women, it can produce an "end of the world" experience. Most of my calls came in between two and three in the morning. I would either meet with the victim at the scene, police station, or hospital emergency room, and was always relieved to see them alive, able to dialogue, and well enough to receive treatment. I will never forget the looks on the faces of parents, uncles, brothers, and friends of the victim. Their pain is second only to that of the victim. Most often the family members want to unload their anger (which is really their pain) by blaming and accusing the victim first, then of course, the perpetrator. This is always wrong, and never allowed, especially when I'm around. Girls, you are never at fault for someone taking you against your will. NEVER, ever, NEVER. The perpetrator is the criminal and not you. The loved ones in your circle are filled with such sorrow and personal pain on your behalf, they often explode and lecture you on why you didn't listen or why you allowed this. Of course, you didn't allow it. Ladies, you have the right to walk around naked on Main Street and no one has the right to rape or assault you. However, I would strongly advise against it.

During counseling, I would allow the victim's loved ones to talk to me initially, in order for their pain to be released on anyone except the victim. It comes out first with anger and resentment, then judgment, followed by a burst of tears and sobbing. They feel their inability to help their loved one, and they cry that out. Everyone gets hurt here....including me. GIRLS...The best protection is for you to be aware of it, practice common sense, listen to your intuition and go with what you hear. Listen to that still, small voice inside you, and if you miss it, pay close attention to those who care about you, and listen to what they're saying. Do not be stubborn on this. Many good fathers have a strong intuition about the men dating their daughters. To the extent possible, see that your date picks you up at home where your family has the opportunity to meet and surmise him. If single, meet in public places. If nothing else, a man with ill intent will know that he has been seen by your family, your loved ones, or in public. I've heard stories of people being drugged, drinking too much, or put into situations they cannot handle. Then the worst kicks in. With date rape, somehow your *no* just doesn't hold up. A bizarre fact is that a high percentage of date rape is perpetrated by "friends" and acquaintances.

A grandmother goes jogging and is attacked; a girl babysitting alone is singled out; an innocent trip to the store at night is an opportunity for mishap, and none of this is through any fault of the woman. Just being female makes you prey for male predators. I am not asking you to live your life in fear, but common sense and intuition are rules to adhere to. Do not risk unnecessary exposure, and seek the right and conventional ways of socializing to minimize risk to your personal safety.

I once attended a rape trial where a young woman had been assaulted and given a common drug in her drink, and became woozy. She couldn't walk or think straight, and was easily manipulated with no will to do anything about it. The guy played it up publicly as being the good guy in caring for her. As he "lovingly" steadied her and carried her to safety, people looked at him with sympathy and admiration. He walked her outside and hailed a cab to personally take her home. He took her to his house first, did the deed, then drove her home. He also took pictures of her for a collection he had going. She awoke the next day with a lot of questions about her body, how she got home, and why she had no recollection of the night before. She knew she had been violated and drugged. Proving it is what the trial was all about, and it wasn't going well. Her past conduct, reputation and behavior all came under examination and public scrutiny. Mind you, she had done nothing wrong. Please...I don't want any more stories to hear or tell.

Girl Pearl: One of the best feelings in the world is to love, admire, and respect someone who you know loves, admires, and respects you just as much.

Stun gun Anyone? Shocking!

California law permits citizens to carry stun guns. It is one of the best kept secrets around, and ladies you are now in on it. Girls, for a price of anywhere from $30 to $100, you can purchase a device that delivers millions of volts right from the palm of your hand and onto the person intending to do you harm, instantly putting an end to any real or perceived threat. All you have to do is touch the person and they go into a fish-out-of-water syndrome. They flip, they flop, their muscles convulse, they shake violently, then crumple onto the ground, remaining incapacitated for anywhere from one to three minutes, depending on the dose. It is during that time you can: jolt them again (optional), start screaming (optional), or make your way to safety and call for help. I came across this years ago, and have shared it with many people who have benefited.

For the past five years, I've dealt with a company called TBO-TECH Self Defense Products, out of Raeford, North Carolina run by my good friends Steve and Jennifer Thibeault. They have excellent customer service, exceptional products, and a great selection. It took some time to find a reliable source I could count on to meet my criteria, and TBO-TECH is that company. You can take your time and have fun shopping on their very impressive website: www.tbotech.com/pearl. Visiting the website is like dying and waking up in self-defense heaven. In addition, they will take your phone calls and discuss with you what product best fits your personal needs. Jennifer is extremely knowledgeable on her products, and prides herself on custom-fitting her customers to their individual needs. In my last phone call with her, she stated she receives calls from both men and women, describing their circumstances and fears, and she recommends the product that corresponds to their individual situation. It's everything you would hope to hear from someone when it comes to the subject of protecting yourself. I often wonder how many of the circumstances might have turned out differently for those I was counseling, if they'd had a stun gun.

Remember, your common sense is still Plan A, and the stun gun is a very effective Plan B. No one expects it will happen to them, which is something the perpetrator uses to his advantage. Having a stun gun protects you from his devious plan for you. My goal is not to have you go through your life in a state of paranoia, but to increase your awareness levels and give you options to protect yourself, rather than be in a situation where you're begging and wishing this wasn't happening. It is similar to having band-aids, safety pins, or chap stick in your purse. When you need these things, you're very glad you have them. Ladies, it is wise to have a backup position in everything you do. Self-protection is no exception.

TBO-TECH products are easy to use and hold, affordable, and fit in your purse or in the palm of your hand. Some are disguised as cell phones and lipsticks, so as not to attract any unusual attention when bringing them out. Holding a lipstick or cell phone in your hand is quite normal and allows you to have it out and ready when you think or suspect a problem is brewing. No harm done if all goes well. You just hang up the phone or put your lipstick away. Now, if you were right, then you're ready to put some of that lipstick on your attacker or offer him your cell phone while you hold it. You get the picture? In my opinion, the more volts the better, because the larger voltage also makes a very intimidating sound. Without fail, each time I've demonstrated this product, people cringe and jump from the noise the sparks give off. Everyone else will be shocked and stunned (pun) just from the sound alone. Even dogs will react with caution to the sound it emits.

I have often observed that the world is not a friendly place toward women. They are more at risk. Remaining unaware or dumb is a choice...don't make that choice. Ladies, go now and let your answer to any threat be shocking to your uninvited guest.

Girl Pearl: *Sometimes being elegant, beautiful and ravishing isn't enough...you may have to be stunning too.*

Living Together May Not Be Living

Despite having argued this subject over and over again throughout the years, and knowing the pitfalls and less than stellar returns, women still continue to honor this dishonorable conduct and give in to the male's request to have something without commitment, and without being responsible or accountable for it. That something is YOU. Let that sink in. Yes, it is possible to make living together work. You can also walk backwards, but then that is not what you were created to do, now is it? I mean no disrespect to anyone who has made this work for them, or to anyone who likes to walk backwards. I just maintain it is working against you, and you don't know it yet. It is also one of those areas you may fear to explore, especially if you really don't want to know the truth about it. By examining and bringing the subject into the light of reality, you may discover how inappropriate the conduct is. Search this out for yourself, so you can modify it while you can. To die realizing that you never lived is a form of hell. To have allowed yourself to live less of a life than the one God intended for you, is not the grand prize. It is the booby prize and you are the booby. The male is the booby maker and taker. I cannot find enough derogatory words to comment on a male who uses, disregards, and diminishes another's life experience. Ladies, why do you allow this to continue?

For those of you considering to live with someone, don't. Let me point out for your consideration some of the difficulties that may arise for you down the line. You may start out with the understanding that this will just be temporary, and you may even give him a deadline, after which he must decide whether to marry or not. Now, you think...*I will make everything so wonderful, that he will want to marry me!* It sounds logical at first glance, but consider that once you move in, you have lost *all* ground, and he has gained all he wants, including the upper hand and the advantage. He has no reason to marry you, because he already has you without an honorable commitment. Be prepared that when your deadline arrives, he will most likely still not be ready to decide, and the onus will be entirely upon *you* to pack up and leave. Will you be able to do this? He's betting you won't, and he's most likely right. The common course of action for a woman to take at this point, is to extend the deadline. It is in just this way that many women end up eight, ten, even twenty years or more down the line, never having the fulfillment of their hearts' desires. They feel incapable of leaving, because by now they've invested a good portion of their youth with this person, and can't imagine going back into the world of dating to begin again. Their first action in *living together,* set them up for their *lack* of action in not being able to leave. For those of you already in this situation, please revisit it and bring some honor to it. Reassess your reasons for doing it in the first place, and ask yourself if you're getting what you wanted, or are you feeling stuck, not able to leave, yet unfulfilled in staying. Also consider asking whether you want to be in the same situation five or ten years from now, because if you decide to stay, most likely you'll still be there then.

Emotionally, mentally and financially it may make sense, but it fails spiritually. Remember, the breath of God is within you. Honor that and everything else is honored. Dishonor it and consequences will follow which you will not be free to choose. Do not take false comfort in the fact that everyone is doing it. First of all, everyone is *not* doing it, just a misguided few. Those who are, have created reasons and surrounded themselves with friends who help reduce the pressure of their own conscience to stop. Second, this is not something you take a poll on. This is between you and your inner conscience. In other words, it's between *you and you.* If you have allowed your conscience to receive programming detrimental to your life's well-being, character, morals, or intuition, then there is a deeper tragedy at work here. How can God honor you for dishonorable conduct? Rewarding inappropriate behavior is backwards thinking, which is exactly what the prince of this world and dark forces specialize in. You cannot serve two sources any more than you can bet on every single horse to win in a horserace, and still make money. You have to choose a horse and bet well, then hope it wins. In life, you must choose a side, and the side you choose must be profitable to you and offer gain, allowing you to evolve.

The need to get out of the parental home or sacrifice yourself for your family's sake is a common reason to move in with someone. But I would ask why you are having, trading, or allowing intimacy (sex) for this. The oldest profession in the world is trading sex for favors. I am sorry to be rude, but to live with someone for those reasons is imitating this behavior. Guys are natural opportunists and can justify that they're making the best of a good opportunity. That's one of the methods they use to offset the message within themselves coming from the still, small voice called *conscience*. When they tire of all the maintenance that comes from this type of living, they'll just look for another female to use. That's how they found you. Ladies, what is in it for you? Answer: heartache and heartbreak.

Girl Pearl: *Ladies, when looking at the role a man should play in courting and dating, consider it as a man applying for the job of loving you for the rest of your life. To know if he is qualified, you must know what those qualifications are.*

Girl Pearl: *At the right time, it is permissible to express one's self in total; namely, with the soul, mind, body and spirit. Even then, the mind adds its music and the emotions their caresses, and still, who knows anyone for real or for all time? Never until you journey within and find the One who assembled all the parts, will you find whole and true contentment.*

V. COURTING, LOVE, MARRIAGE, DIVORCE

Courting is a Ritual

It has been said that *time* reveals all. Yet in today's dating and courting world, this important ingredient is often missing. If you wait patiently for an answer to anything, time will deliver it to you for examination. Works every...*time*. Choosing your course and testing that choice will become clear, reveal itself to you, then continue to lead you as you go. The opposite is true too. In speeding up this process, you take unnecessary risks. We would do well to bring back the formalities of having chaperones, meeting one's parents, friends, neighbors, and having *getting to know you* gatherings which lend support and bring meaning to the courting ritual. Courtship can be, without a doubt, one of the most delightful experiences one can have on this planet and in this lifetime. To meet someone you like and want to see again and again, and for that someone to feel the same way about you, is bliss. When the right two people start this process, they suspend and create a temporary world of their own, where only the two of them matter. It is a wonderful time of awe, daring, and mystery, so extraordinary it produces side effects which are most pleasant. No drug, drink or dream can match its euphoria. The first thing to go is your appetite. Oh, you will dine, but on the experience of being together, and in some cases, while eating less, you actually become weak, but love strengthens you. Another common experience is that time means nothing to the two in pursuit of each other. Traveling to see someone, spending hours and hours together, then realizing it's late and time to leave, happens frequently. You just don't want the experience to end. Then, there is the *wanting to surprise and treat each other in a special way* experience. This is done in such seemingly small ways, yet the real beauty is the pleasure the giver gets by pleasing the receiver, and *both* gain from the experience. Reversing the process allows each to take turns being pleased and giving pleasure. Still another set of joys to be found is in just being silent with each other, and at other times, communicating freely. It is a love paradox. In the first one, you are simply content to be together. If you get to hold hands, embrace, or share anything, the reward for it goes through the roof. In the second one, you talk and listen to each other as if you were truly the only two people on the planet, and no one else existed. You may be in a room full of people, but the moon is in your eyes, and you only see and hear each other. Places that you both visit together take on new meaning. The beach was always the beach, until it became *your* beach, the beach you went to together. Sunsets come and go, but now they were created especially for you two. Movie theatres are now triggers for pleasant memories because you went there together. What the movie was about takes second place. Food...any food shared together, now becomes manna. Here is where I am going with all this. I want to let you in on a little secret which comes by way of questions. Why would you want to speed up this whole process? Why would you want it to end? This experience will never come around in the same way again. It's called *courtship,* and is truly magical in nature. There is a first time for everything, and certainly this is one of the sweetest, most decent experiences known to man (and woman). In later years, you will find yourself saying *remember the time...?*

That being the case, when your time of courtship comes, I want you to suck the marrow out of the experience. Sip it like fine, expensive wine that goes for $10,000 a glass. Treat your time of courtship like your own shooting star, soaring through the heavens on a wonderful secret mission. Drag this ceremony out. Put brakes on it. Be selfish with it and turn it into what you want it to be. Make it extend itself, then pine, swoon and repeat until it hurts exquisitely. This type of pain only comes around once, so take in all you can stand. In the meantime, you are learning about each other, introducing each other to new things, and family and friends can only admire what you've found and how you're going about it. You are on a most pleasant journey that doesn't have to end anytime soon.

Girl Pearl*: To see the love you feel in someone else's eyes is the greatest happiness.*

Nature Does it Too

All that has life, is courting and flirting around the earth without end. Have you ever heard the wild stallion's call to the mare, his mane quivering, and stomping the ground in the terrible glory of his strength? Oh, what mare could refuse that majestic command?

There are the magnificent whales, with graceful balletic ceremonies; other fish puff out, turn colors and dart about; peacocks strut, some birds squawk, some kiss, and others perform elaborate neck movements; insects chirp, and various other creatures croak, babble, howl, hiss, squirm, dance, circle, crawl, make noises and strike poses we find comical, but to their like-kind are serious courting rituals. For this reason, nature becomes the most articulate preacher, whose message to man comes not in words, but in marvelous mysteries; and mysteries not for the *minds* of men, but for their *hearts*, compelling wonder and astonishment through rituals, ceremonies and newness of life. Everywhere, the song of love is carried on the breezes in a thousand forms until it reaches its ends, there to answer and satisfy the true desires of its intended receivers.

In all this...all these exquisite multiplicities of life forms, let us remember that not everyone who participates, necessarily walks away a winner. This makes for an excellent observation related to you. The male attracts and the female responds, and it is she who does the choosing, but only when she is good and ready. The losers (or the un-chosen, to be more kind) must all move on. The system works. There are many species on this planet other than humans which mate for life, who even mourn when their mate is taken from them prematurely. How much more should we, being made in the image of God, stand in reverence of this beautiful ritual of mating for life?

Consider the eloquent example the birds have given us on the subject of dating, waiting and mating, and then bring it closer to yourself. The birds go about their day-to-day routines, and when the right time presents itself, they entertain and interact with each other. In between, they explore their surroundings and live in the world of birds, singing as they go about their business. They need not concern themselves with food, shelter or clothing, for it has been provided. One day, two birds of a feather will come together and court, and when they do, their song of celebration is lifted into the heavens, as a new generation is about to be formed. Without understanding why, they know how to live and make the most of each other's company. It is no wonder that birds were used as an example in the Bible to illustrate the point that they neither reap nor sow, yet they are provided for. The point holds up to this day. Can you see the benefits of living in an uncomplicated way, and how it prospers? Rather than reinventing the wheel, reinvent yourself to turn with the wheel of life.

Eventually, and in good timing, you may want to end this courtship phase, only to begin another, when you both know in your hearts that it is a worthy and good thing to do. Think of a caterpillar who had a good caterpillar life, and now transforms into something it cannot even imagine: a butterfly. So it will be with you when you find your true and intended mate to settle down with. This will involve taking an oath to love and honor one another, which should not be confused with a commitment. An oath is a solemn promise, binding two in such a way that induces the dynamics of the invisible world. (See *The Marriage Oaths* chapter). When you join yourselves to each other in this noble and honorable way, God has no choice but to release his word upon you and chart a new destiny designed for two becoming one. He loves to do so. The rewards and treasures of happiness, joy, contentment and peace are waiting for both of you, and are designed to meet all your needs and exceed your dreams and expectations. Can we agree that God knows how to give good gifts? Yours are magnificent and catered specifically to you. Everyone has a treasure trove waiting to be claimed, which no one else can lay hold of. Please take him up on his wonderful promises, and look forward to this adventure.

Girl Pearl: *Girls, you are a worthy prize, and that unique inner treasure inside called <u>you</u>, is the grand prize.*

The Two Greatest Needs of Mankind

Two very important human conditions came into being for mankind, and by virtue of the fact that both were given to Adam by God, they are inherently in each one of us also. The first: *it is not good to be alone*; and the second: *everyone wants to be loved*. These two conditions have been at work in every human being since creation, but are expressed differently by all. Children who misbehave, in a misguided way, are crying out for these two things. *I need and want attention that I cannot describe or express. Whatever it is, please give it to me!*

Juvenile delinquents are screaming it in their behaviors when they lie, cheat, steal and commit crimes, or act out erratically. They are trying to say they need to be loved, hugged, wanted, needed, told what to do and held accountable in the right way until they understand it. They test others in order to receive their love verifications. Instead, they get a police record for their misguided efforts to be loved.

209

Wives and husbands plead and seek for these two things in their behaviors. A man wants to be recognized and admired for what he is and does. He is capable of amazing feats and accomplishments, and wants the company of a woman to share them with. He will go about it in ways that are not traditional, but he is only saying the same two things: *I don't want to be alone, and I want to be loved.* Here is where looking beyond words to find real meaning takes place. A woman may rebel, argue and even say things she doesn't mean, but when this is understood and interpreted correctly, she is only crying out for those two great needs.

How we go about fulfilling these two fundamental needs, is most important if we are to achieve wholeness and a sense of complete well-being. Shortcuts, experimentation, rushing into situations and being willful, only delay, rob and complicate our progression toward this goal. Girls, instead of unfolding like a beautiful flower, you will spend all your time and energy defending yourself and licking your wounds. Out there is your Prince Charming. He is looking for you, and wants to see your goodness. If he is a prince, then you must be a princess. Are you a princess in waiting? A lady in waiting? A prize to be found? A gift to be unwrapped?

Girl Pearl: *A graceful woman's age is really never that important. That's because her beauty comes from within and can never fade away. She has lined herself up with the stars and they twinkle forever.*

Love: Just What Is It?

It was here before you got here, and will be here after you leave. We also know it's a pleasant, sought after experience and state of being, desired by all who visit this planet. There are many types of love. Even *not hating* is a form of love, albeit a low-level application, but a variation of it, nonetheless. Before it discovers us, however, as we journey and mature, we soon begin to find out what love is *not*. Knowing what it *is* remains elusive to many, because it cannot be understood by the mind. Can color be understood by the blind, or Mozart by the deaf? So it is with love…it must be experienced.

When real love shows itself, the dose and the experience speak for themselves, and the two who are in it need never ask the question: *how will I know when it's love?* The only requirement is to participate and receive. The very beauty of being in love is that both are in it the same way, with equal degrees of vulnerability, emotions and helplessness. It is a place where both *give*, and in freely giving, the inevitable result is that both *receive.* It can be euphoric. It works on a person like a tonic or an elixir. When the two are apart from each other, they experience a pleasant sort of pain, and when together, feel deep contentment, satisfaction and a sense of arrival. Love occupies a great place in the survival of our species. It's a powerful force which allows us to partake of it, gives us the truest understanding of what it means to give and receive, and renders us open and vulnerable for all the right reasons. Oh love, come to me in great quantities, and make haste about it!

As true love is the greatest augmenter of mankind, false love is the greatest corrupter. It comforts and embraces, even while it overwhelms our reason, and robs us of all sensibilities. It will build us up with lies at the same time it pulls us down with truth. The truth of its *deception*, that is. Its ending is unhappy, and will leave you unfulfilled and full of remorse; and when remorse comes calling, it is always late. The very moment in which you accept its lies and deception, is the moment you cease to be your own person. You have surrendered yourself to dark forces for all the wrong reasons, and your battle to gain the high ground will always be hard-fought and without victory, until you are worn down and out. Here's your part: *you knew it was wrong.* Let this sink in, ladies. You knew it because your conscience told you. You will most likely admit this afterward, when you have been snapped back to reality in a very unpleasant way.

This is why we want to extend, support, honor, and bring back the courting period, and then, when you're ready, you'll want to be very sure who you are surrendering your heart and allegiance to. It may benefit the male to move fast and loose, but you are the one that loses in the end if things go south. Why play to lose? When you meet someone who isn't lining up with your standards, you stand to lose that person. But you see, you won't be losing anything, because he brought you nothing to begin with. You outed him and saved yourself a trip to Heartbreak Hotel. Remember, the prince of this world has a marriage plan for you too, a plan you do not want, but one which will *appear* very attractive. It bears repetition that the reason the devil can appear as an angel of light is that his real first impression (horns, tail and pitchfork) doesn't work, but his deception does. If you observe most marriages today, you will see that a very attractive bill of goods has been sold to many, but is not working. By not accepting a lower form of love, you have already won, because you have not given honor to the game by playing it, which constitutes a win for you. By not playing you didn't lose, and by not losing, you won!

Many of us have friends we love, and who love us. A real friend performs in a real way, and will even risk the

212

friendship to preserve the sanctity of it. If this friend saw you drifting from truth or reality, and slowly escaping into a false world, he or she would speak up, tell you the truth, and help you return to your senses. Not only is this a friend to keep, this is the friend you should be, also. Iron sharpens iron, and imagine the benefits that await you by having someone willing to point out your blindside, give you feedback, tell you the truth about yourself, and in doing all this, loving you at the same time. If you are seeking truth, especially the truth about yourself, you will grow by leaps and bounds when you have such a friend. Anyone who doesn't do this, or encourages the opposite, is not your friend, and there is no real love at work either.

While we are on this subject of friendship, consider your circle of close friends. It is a good time to ask yourself *why?* Why did you choose them? Did you choose them because they *go along to get along* with you and your agenda at all costs? Is it because they yield to you and tell you what you want to hear? Or, do they correct you when they see your error? Well? Now, to be very fair, ask the question in reverse: Why did they choose you? Which one are you? Ponder...ponder...ponder...you only have one life. Go for the meaning and the value in all you do, and you will never be sorry.

If you see in a person, a commitment to what is right, true, fair, just, honest, good and beneficial, then you are seeing someone with a love for God and his principles. It is in this way that God will show you the difference between false love and the real thing. Everything we do must be brought into the light of reality to be examined by truth. Your prospective date/mate is no exception. If he is full of a deceiving or beguiling love, you need to know it. You are looking for a true friend and an honest person, first and foremost. Then, this friendship can blossom into many things, love being one of them. Is it so difficult to believe that before you love someone you should like them? Learning to love someone takes time. It's called courting.

If You Don't Like to Argue, Don't Get Married!

I have noticed when counseling people, or even in my marriage via arguments, it may take hours to break through the hard rock and nonsense until we strike the inner gold. Most people don't stay the course, and go the same way they came in, that is, with nothing. If you are going to argue, go full circle and make it mean something. It must have closure. Disagreeing is good. It allows us to explore, test, and refine our beliefs. It also brings into the light those hidden emotions or behaviors you didn't even know were in you, that needed to be exposed. When we do not handle disagreements correctly, we swallow them up and think we are rid of them. We hold them in, and they're gone for the moment, but they are stored up, and not forgotten. We were not designed to store, but to explore and let things pass by and through us. Suppressing and holding onto negative feelings or experiences, causes stress on the organs, and supports a false life. Stop holding things in, and start spitting them out!

Of course, arguing must be done in a constructive way. Being disagreeable or domineering when conversing doesn't work. Anger, or unrestrained, misguided and explosive behaviors will create new problems to be stored up, courtesy of guilt. Guilt comes from wrong choices. Ignoring those wrong choices rather than correcting them, produces compound guilt. So, before, during and after getting to know someone, be advised that disagreements and arguments are part of life and serve a purpose. Command that purpose to serve you, by building and refining your character, showing you what's in you, and making you into a more patient, attractive person. Be aware of the temptation to criticize the other person, using blame as a reason not to look at yourself and your part. You do not need to assess or judge, just listen and observe. We want to learn what to do right, and stop doing the wrong. Be committed to the truth, which in turn makes your motives pure, and great things can happen from there if you stay the course.

Daters, friends, and married couples, before you pull the patience plug and go into your anger and threats rant, you would be wise to make sure everyone knows exactly what you are talking about, and that you, too, understand what is being discussed. Everyone may not be on your page, or you may be the one on the wrong page. You have the power and the opportunity, so take some time out to simplify, clarify, identify, then magnify what you are saying and why. This is the work required to bring about the necessary change one is seeking for a more intimate life and relationship.

Girl Pearl: Women need to teach that the secret to winning an argument with them is very simple: Don't argue!

Marriage and The Marriage Oaths

Well, well, well, we have reached the point where two people want to make life more interesting, more valuable, and easier, by traveling through it with each other. Prepare yourself for great things, because God just eats up any two who set out to become one. Now, we are going to begin a long and fascinating journey, and defining it is a reasonable thing to do. Enter: the oath of office. This is a sworn statement, taken and given intimately by the participants to each other, and is witnessed before men and God, marking the beginning of their journey together. What comes out of a person should be an expression of the heart, if it is genuine, focused, and grounded. An oath is a sacred declaration, binding two together. Its origin has its roots long before men learned to read or write. They uttered, then carried out their utterance. Those who practiced this faithfully became men and women of the highest order, whose oaths were a *living* contract rather than a written one.

Two people taking and giving oaths is one of the most stirring, attractive things to witness or partake in. Every word spoken by the tongue and from the heart of the declarant should be meaningful and solemn. We have all witnessed two people taking marriage vows as part of a ceremony which includes flowers, music, entertainment, dining, dancing, singing, games, gifts and celebrating. I would like to see the oath portion separated from all this. I like the idea of a man going to the woman he has chosen to honor, and committing to her with no distractions, rehearsals or planning, then stating the affairs of his heart to her and swearing them with an oath. The woman would do the same, and this would bind them forevermore, each bouncing themselves off their promises to each other. God will take note of this…he is attracted to people who keep their promises. Customize these oaths to suit yourself:

The Man: *I love you with all my heart and being. I have prayed to God for many things, and he answered quite a few of them when he delivered you into my life. I thank him for answering my prayer specifically on this subject. By honoring you, the one he sent me to travel through life with, I will honor him too. We shall now bond between us, revealing ourselves as we travel, digging deep within each other to mine the gold and prepare a place to receive each other's love. Nothing on earth, can or will, interfere with this promise. Will you join me and help me make a way and a home for us in this portion we call life? If you do, I will protect you, care for you and watch over you all the days of my life, learning as I go.*

The Woman: *You are my chosen, and your love is my delight. I will trust and follow you, and help you in all I am capable of doing. I pledge my devotion to you for all time. My dream of finding you is fulfilled. I will honor you above all other relationships and with my whole heart. I will be company to you, and your intimate confidant. Please be patient with me as you teach me those things that will enhance us both, and lead me into all truth as it is revealed to you. I will care for you with the joy and singing of my heart, and create a place of comfort for us to grow together and thrive. God has answered the desire of my heart.*

Ladies, there are thousands of ways to express what is in your heart. What is important, is that your oath and his should be exchanged intimately and solemnly, in whatever time it takes to share and receive them. You will have a lifetime after that to implement them. Nothing should detract from, or interfere with, this personal exchange. It is a sacred agreement between two in love, and loses intimacy when shared with any third party. Although sharing it publicly or privately is optional, the point is that this oath now declares and binds your lives to each other and to God. It will be tested, but will be strengthened through those tests, and bring the desires of both your hearts to the surface over your lifetime. God wills it so.

Girl Pearl: *Beauty more than bitterness makes the heart break.*

On Two Becoming One

What a deep and fascinating subject this is, and what mystery surrounds it! Look at it objectively. Nothing at all like a man or woman exists in our solar system, and there is reason to believe this is true even in nearby systems. Also, consider how compatible we are to earth and to each other, with no additional supplements or instructions. We were placed here and then told to do what comes naturally to us. First, having a companion in whatever we do is a magnificent concept in and of itself.

The Bible mentions that the two shall leave their mother and father and become as *one*. This is a beautiful mystery, the concept is understandable, yet the dual effort required to accomplish this is ongoing, and at times emotionally painful. Although the rewards along the way make it well worthwhile, it takes years to become compatible with a spouse and develop into this third entity: *one*. The work involved is the cooperative, willing crushing and mitigating of each other's prides and egos. Each becomes less of a god or goddess, and more of a servant to the other, and eventually to God, who will bless this partnership abundantly. There can be no competitive spirit between them, but one of cooperation, each an asset to the other. Then, from pooling what they both bring to each other, the two become a very productive *one*. The man gravitates toward those things which come naturally to his skills and talents, and the woman does the same.

Courting presents an opportunity to investigate, glimpse and practice this process. You will be allowed to see whether you can find common ground to build on, and whether both of you will be able, willing and ready to take on the world, carve out paths, and acquire your portion as one integrated body. What an incredible invitation, that two already unique creations have the possibility of coming together to custom-create a third living organism, which in truth is not at all a third element, no, no, it is infinitely more dear, and more intimate than a party of three…it is *one!* What a beautiful mystery! One plus one is two, and then two are one.

Girl Pearl: *The only thing a woman doesn't tire of is being loved.*

The Affair

Ladies, if you are married or seriously dating someone, you are not allowed to have an affair, and then maintain the title *lady*. Also, you will not get the results I speak of throughout this book if you practice such things. Do not expect to find favor with God or men. You are in uncharted waters when you begin to entertain an affair. It is a risky, selfish, and dangerous thing to enter into. I am no authority on adultery, but I do have understanding of its mechanics, the strong *pull* it can have on a person, and its effects...before, during and after...*the deed*. The wanting of something you cannot, or should not have, has its roots in the Garden of Eden, originating with the fruit of the tree of knowledge of good and evil. God said: *No, you may not have this.* There is something alluring about wanting something you cannot have. It is the same principle with a sign that says: *no fishing.* To a fisherman, this is too good to pass up, because it tells him there are fish there and, after all, he is a fisherman! So it is with pursuing something illicit and out of bounds. While it is allowed (it is called temptation), what do you gain if you engage it? In refusing the tempting goods, what have you really lost? In fact, in that very moment of your refusal, somewhere in the invisible world, your true desires begin making their way toward you without your knowledge.

It is important to re-emphasize that females think with their emotions and ani-males with their body parts. This is the core attraction of the affair. It is animal-based behavior, so we must think this through rationally, inviting our common sense principles into the mix. It does take two, and if one person is irrational or needy, the common sense application will not be allowed to prevail, simply because the two are not on the same page. Consequently one force will pull against the other, resulting in either diving into the affair, or walking away from it. This moment can come subtlety or like a whirlwind. It is temptation at work with dark forces lurking about. If those dark forces prevail, we find what we *think* we are looking for, but it is quite the opposite of what we need. It is the beginning of our downfall. Unconsciously, you are acting out and completing a destructive cycle, invisible to you, but very much alive in you, and starving for life force. It (this dysfunction) wants to live and rule, and it needs you to feed it this dark matter (sin) in order for it to stay alive and grow. If you move forward into this pseudo-exciting arena, in time you will discover, and unhappily pay, the price demanded for doing so. (See: *The Monkeys Paw.*) The empty and temporary payoff you seem to be getting is never worth its consequences, and many have fallen because of it.

Why do you suppose adultery is one of the *Thou shalt not* commandments? It leads you away from the promises and principles of God, and calls down upon you an entirely different set of dynamics where the prince of this world is your mentor, and your flesh has become his student. Your fate is shifted from the hand of God into the hands of the world. Everything God wants to save you *from*, is now upon you, and begins making its claim upon you. Woe unto you. When the thrill is eventually gone, you will clearly see and experience the pain and horror of your choice.

Consider that when the body goes into shock for any reason, it produces natural painkillers to offset the pain of the experience. Your dentist or doctor performs this artificially, to access your body with minimum discomfort to you. When the body comes out of shock, the pain returns until full recovery takes place. So it is with having an affair. Beginning it is alluring, exciting, and imitative of life. All the *wrong* in you comes alive, trying to convince you it is right because it feels good. You know it's wrong because your conscience is telling you so, but you've begun to grow numb to your conscience by entering the world of mind, emotions and reasoning, all of which encourage you to proceed. It never turns out the way you had hoped, and why should it? It was created using dark forces. You were created using light forces. Truly, *you know not what you do* when you enter into this realm. What did you expect to find? Do you actually believe there is joy, harmony, peace, or prosperity in the kingdom of hell? Yet hell is the place you just entered. Why would you go there? It is a place of torment...of short-term pleasure followed by long-term pain. The stories I've heard about Hades is that it's a place of unrest. Don't go there to find out. Believe the stories.

220

While you are operating in this false way of life, your ability to deceive, beguile, cheat, and mislead is drastically enhanced and becomes seemingly all-powerful. At the beginning, the father of all lies will empower you to get you started. During this time you are under the illusion that you can maintain control over it. Yet, the longer you continue, the less control you have, until you are fully hooked and then cooked. After that, you will operate on autopilot, convincing yourself all is well because lightening didn't strike you down to stop you. In the invisible world, however, you have surrendered your soul. You just haven't seen it yet.

Those who have traveled down adultery road, report afterward that the cost of admission was never worth the price they paid later on. Families are destroyed and lost, spouses and children are wounded, and lives are shattered. Yet, going in, no one thinks it will happen to them. Consumed with their desire of the moment, they enter into denial or disregard of all they know to be true and right. People just like you and me come out at the other end with the repeated testimony that their lives were destroyed because of the one decision to enter into that dark and secret world of deception. Remember, adultery is such a shameful act, that many hide it from themselves and others until the day they die. Imagine carrying that baggage around all the days of your life.

If you are, or have been confronted with this temptation, heighten your awareness on the subject and ask yourself: *what does it profit me to experiment recklessly with my life?* A wealth of information is available from family, friends, neighbors, doctors, newspapers, schools and the Internet. Do your own research...seek, knock, ask and educate yourself. For those who have not ventured there, stay out of this arena, and if you are strong enough, please go on record to anyone you know who is engaged in it, to stop right now. Say it just like that: *stop it right now! Knock it off.* Believe me, whether they receive or reject it in the moment, the *soul* of that person has heard you. One day, hopefully sooner than later, that person will thank you, and you will have contributed to doing good in this world.

If *you* are involved in, or contemplating it, *I* am telling you *"No!"* and to cease, desist, and be reckless no more. Begin anew, and treat yourself to a fresh start. (See: *Repentance*) In some areas of life you don't get a second chance, for a variety of reasons. Don't risk this. Learn from those who have gone before you. Make smarter choices, not choices which will complicate and make your life more difficult. I know you want to be loved, cherished, and held. We will go about this the right way or not at all. The Bible calls it righteousness. It may produce short-term pain, but if you stay the course, long-term pleasure is guaranteed. This is a promise from the One who sent you here. I concur.

Girl Pearl: *A true man doesn't make you feel special. He just reminds you that you are.*

Divorce for the Right Reasons

Getting married and getting divorced are no joking matters, and both should be contemplated carefully and seriously before entering into either. Attorneys, judges, parents and counselors, along with well-meaning friends and family, induce us to travel the wide, well-trodden road when it comes to solving marital problems or considering divorce. If you are not willing to guide your own ship through the ups and downs of the storms, there are those who will be glad to get involved to do it for you. It is wise to seek sound advice from someone whose life you respect, but you must ultimately make your own decisions, chart your own destiny, take hold of your own helm and guide your own rudder. You must seek the narrow road on this subject. The narrow road is where you and God travel together intimately, and there is no room for anyone else.

222

Considering our uniqueness as individuals, and *then* considering how much more unique a situation becomes when we're paired with another, how can any third party friend or family member fully understand the dynamics between two people, when the two involved don't even understand them? This is why there are trained professionals in this field to give help and feedback, guidance and counseling. Many also turn to church or religious organizations for help navigating through complex and emotional situations.

Family members getting too much involved is, of course, a common mistake. Mothers-in-law often make this critical error when siding with their children, using their emotions and biases. That is the insult, and the injury kicks in when the couple makes up, then both resent the intrusion from mom. Family members, although often the closest to us, are, for that very reason, the least objective sources of help. It is wise to share and seek out solutions for any trouble you are having, but you must use wisdom and discretion in doing so. Lend everyone your ear and not your mouth. In other words, don't contribute too much, but listen to all that is said. This will ensure less of a mess for you down the road. What goes on between two people in marriage or divorce is a very private and complicated affair, and with very few exceptions, should remain that way. One exception is when you are seeking help because you realize you are not functioning correctly or have reached an impasse. Another is when you have baggage you brought to the marriage from your childhood or past, which has begun to show itself. Under these circumstances, discussing with a third party the private matters of the heart which come up between two people, makes sense.

What are valid, righteous reasons to seek a divorce? Here are a few: He is mentally, physically, psychologically, or emotionally abusive; he is practicing infidelity; he is using drugs or alcohol. Ladies, if the spouse is a louse, this is not an acceptable reason. You will have to work things out. This makes my point about dating and waiting. All this should come out during the dating and courting phases, and be handled by either terminating the relationship or working out the problems before you progress to marriage. Once you are married, you must do the work. No perfect recipe exists. Remember, anything worth having is worth working for. Neither of you is perfect, and issues will come up that, if handled correctly, will cause you to learn and grow in stature. Life is one mysterious journey for each of us, and no two travelers will have the same experience. That thought alone is amazing.

If divorce is the road you choose, then a large time-out must follow. Resist the temptation to jump into another relationship. This is an error, a common one, and very unhealthy. A responsible time-out is necessary to assess, recover, unlearn and begin again. Taking time to learn why your relationship failed, and to see your part in it, is necessary so that whatever caused this disruption is indentified and dealt with. I am not talking about the obvious, either. Your pride will convince you and offer support to your ego that it was anyone's fault but yours, and if you did play a part, it was a small one. Let it be known that when it comes to human failures, the humans involved are to blame. So, while it is tempting to blame the guy, please don't, even though you have a very good understanding of his failure. Each party has the responsibility to look at their own part as to why it failed. You played a part too, from beginning to end, and you must confront the part you played with introspection and honesty, as to whether it was dysfunctional, indifferent or just plain ignorant. I am referring to cause and effect. You played a part, and if you don't seek this out so it can be corrected and eliminated, it will follow you into your next relationship as sure as a baby chick follows the mother hen.

The time has also come to reflect on the possibility that you had your own way when you got married. That was *your* way you went, remember? Had you sought peace on the subject via dating and waiting, a different ending would have come into play. Were you so deeply "in love" that you rushed forward with your own plan without consulting and obeying your conscience on the matter? Did you override your conscience when it spoke? Did you ignore all the red flags which are now only too obvious in hindsight? This is the time to be mercilessly honest with yourself in the solitude of your quiet time. Ask questions of yourself (your conscience), which are pertinent to your own circumstances, then answer them honestly, and carefully examine those answers. When truth comes toward you during these times with its gentle whisper, be careful not to brush it away. Tune into it, desire it, be responsive to it and be grateful for it by listening, going toward it and allowing it to reveal your own hidden motives. Desire more of it at all costs, no matter how painful it may be. Seek out all it is trying to show you about yourself, and once you see it, suffer, suffer, suffer for truth's sake, and let it sting you until it finally soothes you like cool water on a muggy day.

Women who avoid doing this work, often enter into the next scenario using opposite strategies, meaning they look for the exact opposite of the man they just separated from. What they don't realize is that opposites are linked to each other similarly to like-kind being attracted to like-kind. What happens too often, is that if you married a weak male, you will now look for his opposite, a strong male. But you will still get a man connected to the original problem, only in another way. If you married a strong male, you may look for a less than strong one which is like ending up where you started. You see, you are still using the same scale of strong and weak. Why use any scale at all? True identities get stolen and manipulated through trauma, shock, and resentments, and cause people to either conform or rebel to their unhealthy circumstances. Imagine two horns on a mean goat, one named "conform" and the other named "rebel." In the end, no matter which horn you choose, it is the same old goat you go home with. You really don't want anyone that is compensating one way or the other. How about someone who is just being himself and not reacting to anything? To rush back into a relationship now, you will only find that the names of the characters have changed, and the circumstances have been altered, but you are beginning another nightmare, where the underlying problem is the same. What then? Time-out. The last thing you need right now is another male. Discover the part you played in all this, have a long, hard look into yourself, then get a handle on your problem and solve it once and for all. If not, you may find in your next relationship, that you have leaped out of the frying pan and right into the fire.

Also, before you consider getting involved again, whether you realize it or not, you have become very vulnerable, and in this condition, you are convenient prey for ani-male predators. You're feeling either rejected or that you failed, you're hurting and wanting reassurances that you are still desirable. You may feel the temptation to prove to yourself that you are attractive to men by testing it. This combination makes you extremely vulnerable. Rise above these animal tendencies and get it right this time. Nail this thing already. You are looking for the deepest, most rewarding experience, not another painful one. As you search for it, remember this very important rule: you must have a place to put it once you find it. Work on that place. It is right there inside of you.

Now ladies, please understand that there will be a tremendous pull and push on your entire being to blame, explain, payback, persecute, and judge, which is in addition to your own pain, loss, and your whole world being turned upside down. Crying, sobbing, weeping, spending time with the right friends and family will help you release your feelings in a constructive way. Holding things in is not an option. This can cause compound resentment which will lead to hate, and the hater is the one who suffers most. While you are busy hating, your real self goes neglected and every moment is tainted, robbing you of God's blessings that come in every nano-second of the day. You must vent it out. You will be angry, and anger comes from the judgment you are passing on this situation. Right or wrong, stop judging, analyzing, or criticizing it. Just get it out, then reach the point where you are not causing yourself to think about it as much. Eventually, and in time, it will reduce itself to where you are able to handle it properly, then you will have victory over it as it comes under your control.

You may be in a situation where you know divorce is necessary due to infidelity or other abuses, but you have not been able to actually begin the process. Truly, the circumstances of divorce can be overwhelming at the very least, and you may feel you are not able to bear the pain and complexity of it, so you put it off and remain in an unhealthy limbo, between somewhere and nowhere, an ambiguous existence. But to remain in this is long-term suffering. It is a slow death. Although you are attempting to avoid the suffering related to divorce, if you are continuing in this unrighteous situation, you are *already* suffering greatly, but it is all for the *wrong* reasons. Go *toward* the very pain you are trying to avoid. Take action by pursuing what you know is right, and you will suffer, to be sure, but your suffering will be for the *right* reasons. When you step out of an unrighteous situation for righteousness sake, help will come to you by virtue of the fact that you took the first step toward the right way. Prioritize, reflect, get some counseling, and discover your blindside. In this mode, you'll be given answers and will set up your journey toward taking the next step, whatever that is.

There will be great emotional and mental suffering with this. Though it is hard to realize, this kind of suffering is good. Suffering for the right reasons is a necessary part of life. The little chick pecking its way out of a shell is in pain and suffering, but soon to be rewarded for it. So is the seed that goes into the ground. It will suffer and crack open, fight the soil and the elements to make its way above ground and into life. In both examples, it is the light that draws them toward it, and compels them to continue. There is a ray of light that beckons you, also. The pressure and stress applied to a piece of coal produces the diamond, and the irritating piece of sand in an oyster produces a pearl over time. So it is with you and your circumstances. They can make you stronger and richer, and while they may appear to be threatening and unsolvable, that is not the case at all. Remember, we were not put here to be defeated, and when we take the first baby step in the right direction, all of heaven and earth comes to assist us. Consider also, that the bullfighter, who gets in the ring with a strong bull, is moving closer to becoming a matador.

We must accept that suffering is part of life, and if we are suffering for the right reasons, it is to our benefit. I am reminded of Jesus and how he suffered. He said those who followed him (in suffering) will not be sorry. Then, I think of what the poet Thoreau said, that *most men lead lives of quiet desperation*. These are two distinctly different types of suffering. In Thoreau's example, you get nothing for it, except to go to the grave with that song of suffering in your heart. Whereas in Jesus' suffering, something good and wonderful comes out of it. Suffer for the right reasons and let's move on. You will be going through withdrawals and unlearning. This takes time. Also, certain phases of recovery, such as anger, blame, guilt, sorrow, and repentance will come. Let them come, and go toward them when they do. They will only make you a better person. You are becoming the diamond and the pearl. In time, you will recover sufficiently to venture back into the dating mode.

As you approach this matter, if children are involved, do not include them in your problems. They are children for only a brief time...let them remain in the world of children. No child should bear the weight of adult problems, so let's not take away the innocence from that arena. Therefore, do not ever, under any circumstances, malign or vilify their father. Resist this temptation at all costs and for all time, because it is just that: temptation. If you are doing it, stop. You are out of control, your misery wants company, you're inflicting *your* damage on the innocence of your children, causing *them* damage, trauma and injury, and it is one of the cruelest, most self-serving acts known to man. Great injury will be suffered by your children, as well as yourself, should you venture down this road. Even worse, and what you may not realize now, is that by doing this, unconsciously, you are sabotaging your future relationship with your children. *Never* do this. If you do, the children will later learn to resent you, no matter how bad the father may be, because a child cannot help but love its parents. Even if your children later agree that you were right about him, they will resent you for having added to their affliction by putting them in the middle. If you were successful in swaying them to your "side" you will lose in the end, because they will have guilt in later years, that they took sides against a parent. They may also resent even your being right about him, because you were still wrong in divulging it to them.

In the grace, patience and suffering it takes to *not* do this, you possess your soul. Yes, you will suffer, because you know things about the man your children will never know. In your suffering, remember: *the years teach much that the days never knew.* In the passage of time, what is necessary for your children to see, will be revealed to them by God through their own life circumstances and situations. When this happens, they will realize you loved them more than you loved yourself, because you did not exalt yourself by berating their father when it was in your hand to do so.

Allow them access to their father, providing there is no reason not to do so. The child needs the love and support of the two that brought them into the world. Explain truthfully (if necessary), in child's terms, and not in detail, what took place. Make it brief and unemotional, avoiding unnecessary and/or intimate details. They may ask questions at the time or later, and you will handle the questions with grace, simplicity, truth and maturity. Perhaps family and friends can help with this process. Leave as much emotion out of it as possible. You do not want to energize or accentuate the negative. Be careful not to project blame, doubt, or fear. Get composed and then proceed. If a direct question is asked, and a truthful answer would "indict" their father, you have the option to refer them to their father for the answer. This way, you have remained truthful, but did not reveal something that would ruin him in their eyes. Your children, unless they are very young, will understand and respect what you have done, even in that very moment, whether you realize it or not.

There is no doubt it is a lot to take on, but you will rise to this occasion. The instinctively maternal part of you is capable of all the amazing things you have heard and read about. Mothers will fight off any circumstances to protect their children, and they are empowered to do so. This power is no respecter of persons, and will come to your aid if you hold no resentment and if you do not interfere with it. Now, we must go about the business of living life, raising children, and in some cases pursuing an income. You must do whatever is required as it comes up, so prepare yourself to get used to operating in a problem/solution mode until your situation shifts.

The Island Test

Before considering divorce for the right reasons, couples should be ordered to spend three months alone together on Reality Island. Believe me, selfish and vain pettiness would soon be replaced by depth, meaning, and companionship gains.

Imagine you and your husband on a deserted, secluded island. You would not find time to criticize, argue, or work against each other, but to the contrary, you'd feel grateful that you were not alone. You would be discovering your strengths and skills together, and putting them to work for the common good of your basic survival. Your needs would be self-evident, and to practice with each other what is right and beneficial would kick in automatically as you went about your daily tasks. There would be nothing negative about it. Both of you would pursue with joy the building of a hut and the gathering of food, with the zest and zeal that come from the pleasure of having a companion in the doing of it all. What is there not to like? It would be the adventure of two explorers, each one glad they were not alone. The *two becoming one* would surely take place, and great things would happen. Even adversity would be faced and challenged together, and would strengthen the union.

Somehow, when all this gets transferred to city dynamics, temptations and complexities of life enter in, and these, along with untested beliefs, set us up to fail. Having too many choices complicates things, and instead of being led by innocence, or the child in you, the adult takes over and unintentionally makes it complex. The child in us doesn't like

231

complexity, but gets things done by keeping them simple and having fun at the same time. The adult in us likes to proceed with caution, think things through, and test the waters before committing. A happy medium between the two brings about optimum results, but to discover the perfect balance takes time and observation.

Water seeks its own level, and so will you. Eventually, you will want the child in you to come out and play more than the adult. Remember, when you were born, this was your default nature.

As you grow older and closer to your exit, it will (or should) become your default nature again. Besides, all work and no play makes you a dull person.

Girl Pearl: My wife is one of the best women on this Continent, although she isn't always gentle as a lamb with mint sauce.

- Artemus Ward

Conclusion

We started this book with a very important subject and have ended it the same way. That subject is YOU the woman, the girl, and the co-steward of this planet. If creatures from another world would have contact with man, I believe with all my heart they would be intrigued and fascinated with him. I further believe that when they met the feminine species, woman, they would be in awe. Placed side by side, they would see the potential and deliberate sense of the man and the woman being here and coming together. When we are not busy answering their questions, they would be busy answering all of ours, because we would hold their masculine representative in similar high esteem and their feminine representative in wonderment. Any work you spend on yourself to become a better person and, by doing so, find a companion with the same ideals, can only lead to one conclusion: deep love and respect for yourself, for others, and for God. Thank you.

The Pearls' Series

Welcome to the Pearls' Series of practical books, designed specifically for you, the Reader. The author has put together three books on important subjects...*must knows* if you are to reach optimum and receive your portion in this brief life experience. We begin with:

LIFE, by introducing *Pearls for the Soul,* a collection of over 800 positive and uplifting sayings that can change the way your day and even your life is going. *Turn to any page....it's for you...*is the mantra of those who glance through it! Now, as to our next subject, the argument continues as to who would benefit more on a subject that involves 3.5 billion people on this planet:

WOMEN: *Pearls for Girls, Dating, Waiting & Sex...In Seeking Cupid...Don't be Stupid,* takes the woman's position in all she aspires for, by supporting, nurturing, then helping to bring about the desires of the feminine heart. Women from 13-60 will not be disappointed, and no subject is spared. Men, you don't have to be left behind either. Order your copy now too. Following this important subject would be difficult, if the next subject wasn't reserved for the Guest of Honor:

GOD: *The Pearl of Pearls GOD I AM Do you know him..?* Whether you do or don't know God, or perhaps are not sure, the most important subject of all is submitted to you for consideration. Man is remarkable, and the *man-maker* defies description. We know him by his works, and all you have to do is open your eyes and behold...whether or not you understand anything is not important. Just don't deny what you see and hear, and you will not be disappointed. The purpose of life is to live a life of purpose. The secret to life is not a mystery, and never was, because trillions have been let in on it. God wants to be found by you....willingly and because you want to know him.

He promises to make your inquiry and your journey worth your while. Take him up on it!

The *Pearls' Series* is designed to assist its readers in being fulfilled, to travel well and deep, and to have a unique story to tell of your adventure.

I will see you amongst the stars, and I will know you by the gleam in your eye....

Richard Alan Naggar

Please inquire by visiting pearlsforthesoul.com

Girl Pearl: *Women are not riddles or puzzles to be solved, but an adventure to be lived with...*